Law School
UNCENSORED

LAW SCHOOL UNCENSORED

Everything You Need to Know
to Survive (and Thrive) at Law School

THOMAS E. LADEGAARD, ESQ.

WORLDCHANGERS
MEDIA

Disclaimer: This is a work of nonfiction. The publisher and the author make no representations or warranties of any kind with respect to this book or its contents, and assume no responsibility for errors, inaccuracies, omissions, or any other inconsistencies herein. The content of this book is for informational purposes only and is not intended to diagnose, treat, cure, or prevent any condition or disease, including mental health conditions. Nor is it intended to substitute for professional advice, including legal advice. You understand that this book is not intended as a substitute for consultation with a licensed attorney. The use of this book implies your acceptance of this disclaimer.

At the time of publication, the URLs displayed in this book refer to existing websites owned by the author and/or the author's affiliates. WorldChangers Media is not responsible for, nor should be deemed to endorse or recommend, these websites; nor is it responsible for any website content other than its own, or any content available on the internet not created by WorldChangers Media.

First paperback edition: October 2024
Paperback: 978-1-955811-74-3
E-book: 978-1-955811-75-0
LCCN: 2024917475

Edited by Bryna Haynes and Paul Baillie-Lane
Cover design and layout by Bryna Haynes
Cover artwork by StockVector via AdobeStock
Author photo: Marcy Browe

Published by WorldChangers Media
PO Box 83, Foster, RI 02825
www.WorldChangers.Media

CONTENTS

Part IV

Part V

LAW SCHOOL UNCENSORED

INTRODUCTION

IF YOU HAVE BEEN accepted into a law school and are awaiting your first semester, or if you're preparing to take the Law School Admission Test (LSAT), you are likely experiencing fear of the unknown. Fear creates anxiety and erodes confidence. If you know what to expect at law school, and therefore become empowered by knowledge and less intimidated by the process, fear will be removed from the equation. If fear is not a distraction, you will focus and retain information better, and you have better potential to be a high-performing student.

While I'm not the first person to educate on law school success strategy, my underdog status gave me a unique perspective. My LSAT score was terrible. I also had mediocre grades in college (more about that later) and was barely accepted to a bottom-tier law school. In fact, this school considered me such a risk that I was placed in mandatory tutoring before the first semester began. I decided to embrace the process and welcome the challenge. In fact, being an underdog inspired me to succeed against the odds, and I went on to outperform my classmates with scholarships.

One of my professors in the orientation program taught me how to be a law student. He explained how law school is a different game from our prior educational experiences. I figured this professor knew what he was talking about, and I bought in—all-in. I applied the system he taught me in every class during my three years of school. This system kept me grounded, focused, efficient, and effective. I'm sure my intelligence and work ethic would have taken me far, but the system launched me toward the top of my class. I therefore graduated in the top 19 percent of my class in a top-tier school despite my mediocre grades and bad LSAT. I also passed the bar exam on my first try. At the time of this writing, I have been a practicing attorney for over twenty years.

In this book, I will share my personal system for law school success so you can adapt it to your own needs and leverage it toward your own professional goals. As I mentioned above, none of this is a "my way is the best/only way" approach. This book details a system that worked for me, and reasonable minds can (and likely will) differ. I won't bore you with statistics, extensive research, or other people's information; I'll just tell you what I saw, what I did, and why it worked—and then, it's up to you to integrate and implement my teachings.

I will also do something far more challenging: I will curb my ego and my desire to want to look good, and instead be authentic and vulnerable in sharing both my successes and my mistakes. I hope it makes for an engaging read.

Part I of this book is directed toward prospective law students. It will challenge you to ask why you want to be a lawyer, dispel some myths about the profession, and provide an honest and blunt assessment to help you decide whether law school is a fit for you. Before you start applying to law schools, you should be able to answer the questions in this section with conviction, and without hesitation. If you can't articulate why you want to attend law school, or if your answers aren't actually about you—for example, your parents told you that you're "good at arguing," you're riding out a bad economy and want to delay entering the job market, or you think you can't make a paycheck as an artist—this section will help you save your money and your time.

Part I also discusses the critical mindset of a law student and the ideal attributes for law students. You may feel like I'm describing you personally, or you may feel like I'm describing a crazy person.

Part II discusses how to get accepted into law school. We will discuss the admissions process so you can efficiently direct your efforts as an undergraduate and maximize your potential for getting accepted to the school of your choice. You will also learn what to expect in the application process, and how to craft a strategy for being accepted into law school.

Parts III and IV are about the law school experience from orientation to graduation. Law school is a totally different game than any other educational experience; in fact, it's so different from college that you will have to relearn how to be a student. What worked for you in high school and college will probably not serve you well in law school. This can make for some harsh realities, and some harsh blows to your ego. All law students are intelligent, accomplished, and ambitious overachievers; those things will no longer set you apart, as it may have in your university days. In addition to the mental adjustments, you will learn a bit about basic legal analysis (how lawyers think and argue) and the first-year curriculum. Equally important, you will learn how to deal with professors who can be intimidating and condescending. Once you settle in, learn how the game is played, and adjust to the pace, law school will be far more enjoyable and satisfying for you.

To be clear: this book is not a run-down of the glories of

the legal profession. Nor is it an attempt to convince you to go to law school so you can dutifully fulfill family, cultural, or societal expectations. It certainly isn't an attempt to get you to "follow my ten infallible steps to success." If you want to preserve your inner image of the TV-drama, sugarcoated experience, this book is not for you. In fact, my goal is that, by the time you finish reading this book, you will have more reasons not to go to law school than you will have reasons to do so.

If you close this book feeling disheartened or dissuaded, good. Law was never the right path for you. You can thank me later for saving you three years of your life and six figures in student loans.

However …

If, when you've finished reading and have assessed the full scope of what your law school dream will entail, you still have that fire in your belly to do right by yourself, your ambitions, and the people you will someday serve …

Then, my friend, you will be ready to tackle law school like a champ.

What I Expect from You

There's a lot of actionable information in this book. I've done my best to make it a fun, easy read with stories of my personal experiences, while still keeping it heavy on substance.

However, reader, there are a few things you need to bring to the table to get the most out of our time together.

First, be open to examining what you "know" is true. The ability and willingness to question everything—including yourself, your motives, and your strategies—will serve you well in every area of life, but also make you a better student and lawyer (lawyers are lifelong students). Although none of us will ever truly get there, objectivity and creative non-attachment are states to which we should all aspire.

Second, feel free to argue with me. As I've shared, this is a book about my experiences, my strategies, and my perspectives. I fully believe that the system I will share with you was the single most important determining factor in my success as a law student—which is why I am committed to passing it on. However, you and I are different people, so feel free to practice those lawyerly skills of dissent.

And finally, regardless of where law school takes you, stay true to yourself. Staying true to your own ethical and moral compass is critical in the legal profession, and your career as a lawyer begins in school.

Let's get started.

Part I

Chapter 1

IS LAW SCHOOL RIGHT FOR YOU?

THROUGHOUT HIGH SCHOOL and college, I supported myself by working in restaurants as a kitchen manager. Nobody can tell me that food service isn't a challenging career. Cooking requires backbreaking labor, long hours on your feet, inevitable injuries from cuts and burns, multitasking abilities, and critical stress management skills. I loved my work and took great pride in it, but I would come home exhausted every night. I also didn't see a great financial future in that career path.

One evening (okay, early morning), after I'd collapsed on the couch, I tried to envision myself as a middle-aged cook, or even a top-notch chef. I couldn't do it. Given the physical demands of the job, I was already flirting with burnout—and I was still in my early twenties. This was obviously a problem.

More, I didn't feel like the work had significant meaning for me. Running an efficient kitchen gave me a sense of pride, and it was nice to receive the occasional compliment from a satisfied customer. However, I couldn't see how perfectly prepared plates and nice presentation could affect anybody's life in a meaningful way. I knew I had a higher calling to help people and positively impact their lives—and it wouldn't hurt to make a decent living at the same time.

My childhood dream was to be an actor. I've always loved entertaining people. But that wasn't on the list of realistic career moves for me, either.

Then, I thought, "Why not become a lawyer?"

I already had great organizational and leadership skills from my years in the kitchen. I loved to learn. And I figured that a courtroom would be a great place to channel my inner actor. It was pretty much the perfect plan. I wanted a career that would be intellectually challenging, fulfilling, and financially rewarding.

And that, my friend, is how I decided to go to law school.

Now, it's your turn.

Why Do You Want to Be a Lawyer?

If you cannot answer this question easily off the top of your head, or if you feel hesitation or equivocation, I encourage you to put this book down and take some time for serious introspection.

If you want to succeed in law school, it will require your total commitment. It doesn't matter what your reasons are for choosing a career in law, or if they sound anything like mine. Just be honest and authentic, because if your reasons aren't strong enough, they won't be able to carry you through when things get tough. And they will get tough.

When I told my grandfather that I wanted to go to law school (and asked for his support with tuition), he said, "Yes, it will be good to have a lawyer in the family."

That took me aback. It didn't matter so much that I would be the lawyer, only that the family had one. I didn't take this personally, as my grandfather had always been supportive of me pursuing my education and dreams, and had never commented on my previous work choices. However, it did stand out to me that this particular career was something he thought would reflect well on the family.

When I got to law school, I met a lot of people who were there for the wrong reasons—and family pressure was top among those reasons. I can tell you from personal experience: you should not enroll in law school to please others. I don't care if your family has generations of lawyers and you had a toy gavel in your crib. If you are going to survive the challenges of law school, you need a burning desire to do this for yourself. Parental, social, or cultural expectations won't be enough. You'll need an internal red-hot burning desire to become a lawyer. If you're primarily doing it to please others, you will lack a sufficient "big why" to get you through the challenges ahead.

Also, it's worth noting that a career in law is ultimately about service. If you're not in it to actually help people—and by people, I mean your future clients—it's unlikely that this path will be fulfilling for you. Everything you will do in this career will be for the benefit of your clients, whether they are individuals, companies, or governmental agencies. Clients will come to you with legal problems, and they will rely upon your education and experience to fix those problems. Depending on your practice area, you will encounter clients in varying periods of distress and uncertainty, and they will expect you to be the steady hand to guide them through the darkness and deliver results. Your job as an attorney is to use your intellect and knowledge of the legal system to help people and companies through some of their biggest challenges. If this sounds like fulfilling work to you, you're in the right place.

With this in mind, I encourage you to create a short, succinct mantra that you can repeat whenever someone asks why you are choosing to go to law school. Mine was, "I am enrolling in law school because I want a career that is both meaningful and challenging." The more I said this, the more important it felt to me to follow through on my decision, because I did indeed want a career that was meaningful and challenging.

Dealing with Naysayers

There are plenty of people in your life who will be enamored with the power, prestige, and income potential of your future career in law. There will also be many who will try to dissuade you. For example, after making my decision to attend law school, I met with my Philosophy of Law professor, a retired criminal defense attorney and former dean of admissions at a prestigious law school. He was an intimidating presence and well-respected throughout the Philosophy Department. I'd taken his class earlier in my senior year and figured he could provide some guidance.

I showed Professor Averbuck my transcript and stated my desire to attend the University of San Diego School of Law. He made no effort to spare my feelings when he reviewed my transcript. In fact, he literally cringed as he uttered: "You got a C in Ethics?" (The emphasis he placed on the word "ethics" really twisted the knife.)

In my defense, I hated the Ethics professor and the class reminded me of high school. I also had a D in another required course in the Philosophy major. While low grades in your major (especially in Ethics) look bad to a prospective law school, I wasn't giving up. My university had a policy that re-taking a class erased the prior grade, so I put in the work and turned that D into an A.

During the same year, a Communications professor asked about my post-graduate plans and then about my GPA (which was good but not great). When I told her, she responded, "You're going to *law school*?"

Italics do no justice to the scorn in her voice. I'm sure the intent behind her spontaneous bloviation was that I should spare myself the pain and disappointment and not bother to apply. However, no professor before or since has inspired me to work so hard. I made damn sure I came out of her class with an A. This professor later recommended me as a tutor for a struggling student of hers.

When I announced my ambitions to my roommates, they had even less enthusiasm than my professors. They found every reason to tear me down. I can see now that my ambition made them uncomfortable and resentful. It wasn't my fault that my goals highlighted their lack thereof—but in that moment, their lack of support really hurt.

Some people make it their business to sow seeds of doubt. These might be people you love and respect, and their negativity might cause you to seriously question your aspirations.

This isn't necessarily a bad thing; as Socrates said, "The unexamined life is not worth living." But there's a difference between genuine concern and naysaying.

Naysayers are like crabs in a bucket who pull down other crabs as they try to crawl out. Some people are truly committed to their mediocrity and get triggered by anyone with goals and dreams bigger than their own. Others, like my professors, have "seen it all," and have fixed ideas about what is and is not possible. I would be living a much different life today if I had listened to these professors or my roommates, and I'm fairly certain that my life would have be filled with regrets and "what ifs."

Once you vocalize your intention to attend law school, the naysayers will make themselves known. If you are truly committed to this path, you cannot let those people undermine your confidence. Let your naysayers motivate you to try harder. The best possible revenge against your naysayers is to achieve massive success. (That said, while negative inspiration can be powerful, it is also fleeting, so you'll also need that internal well of inspiration to keep you going in the long term.)

There is nothing wrong with debating the pros and cons of applying to and enrolling in law school or examining the downsides of pursuing a legal education. Thinking deeply about this endeavor before you start is healthy and constructive. If your discussions with the people in your life are focused on the risks and realities of attending law school, those are necessary conversations to have. If those conversations descend into reasons why you can't or won't succeed as a student or lawyer, or how law school or the bar exam are "too hard," you can and should disregard such advice.

Is Law School Worth the Price?

Warning: the following section contains dire, depressing, and sobering realities.

There's more to your decision to enroll in law school than your burning desire to become a lawyer. There are financial considerations that you must address before making your final decision.

I don't share this information to dissuade you (I'm not a naysayer!), but rather to help you plan, and to test that conviction we discussed earlier in this chapter. If you're unwilling to surmount these challenges, that's a good indication that law school isn't the right path for you.

To estimate the true cost of attending law school, you must consider the following: tuition, school expenses, student loans, the cost of living, and your inability to work during the first year (also known as 1L). Add to that the uncertainty that you will even make the cut and become a 2L (and if you do, whether you will be able to earn a living wage as a clerk during the craziness of that year), whether you can actually pass the bar exam, whether you can find a job with a livable salary ... well, you get the picture. You will need to weigh these financial risks and commitments against your burning desire to become a lawyer. If you finish this chapter with that desire intact, you will have survived a crucial test.

Law school is an expensive endeavor. Unless you are one of the few whose expenses are fully paid by parents, relatives, or the lottery, you will face some difficult realities. In 2022, annual tuition at my alma mater, the University of San Diego School of Law (aka, USD), was $62,200. That did not include summer school. Nor did it include the thousands of dollars in related costs for students, such as books and transportation. When you add in the cost of actually living in or near San Diego, and the fact that you can't (or at least shouldn't) work the first year, you're looking at a six-figure investment.

Even if you're fortunate enough to have a scholarship and substantial savings (which, let's face it, is not the reality for most people entering law school), you will graduate with substantial student loan debt. The debt maintenance can easily equal a mortgage payment, and it is non-dischargeable in bankruptcy; this ups the pressure to pass the bar and find a well-paying job. However, most law firms hiring newly minted lawyers are looking for bargains, as young associates are a dime a dozen. In fact, according to ZipRecruiter, the average entry-level lawyer's salary in 2022 was just under $54,000—the equivalent of about $27 an hour.

Paying student loan debt on a salary like that won't be easy. You can temporarily defer your student loan payments for up to three years if you encounter hardship, but interest will continue to accrue, and you will have to start paying eventually. You can obtain deferment for unemployment, but you will have to provide evidence that you are not employed full-time and that you have been denied full-time employment.

Your student loans can actually be canceled—but only if you join the Peace Corps, the military, or law enforcement, or if you become a teacher, nurse, or counselor in Head Start or a family services agency. In other words, if you want your debt canceled, you must choose a low-paying public service career that doesn't require a law license.

You will likely assume some additional debt while studying for the bar exam. Once you graduate, you are no longer a "student" and become ineligible for federal student loans. However, studying properly for the bar exam will take months of full-time preparation. (A word from the wise: don't even try working while studying for the bar.) Private loans, known as "bar loans," are available to cover your cost of living, the bar review course (about $4,000), and the exam fee. My bar loan was $8,000—but unlike my student loans, it could not be deferred or consolidated. Also, unlike my student loans, it had a variable interest rate which climbed to almost 10 percent within a year.

I was lucky enough to graduate law school with just $73,000 in student loans, not including my bar loan. With interest so outrageous on the bar loan, I prioritized paying that debt, and managed to zero out the balance about six years after graduation. However, that required periodically deferring my student loan debts. Today, nearly twenty years later, I still owe around $36,000. However, I have a manageable monthly payment because I have consolidated my loans. This has allowed me to prioritize and pay off other debt obligations. The payment itself isn't a stressor for me, but those loans are still a consideration when applying for a mortgage, buying a car, or doing anything that factors a debt-to-income ratio.

Now, to be clear, everything I described above is what you will be looking at if things go right.

If you don't make the cut after your first year and find yourself having to choose between repeating your first year or calling it quits, your law school isn't going to refund or discount your tuition.

If you graduate into a bleak job market, you might need to wait tables, tend bar, or get another job outside of the legal industry to make ends meet. This is very common.

Employers also might exploit your plight by offering below-market salary, or even nothing at all, by labeling you as an "intern." Other firms might improperly designate you as an "independent contractor" (a practice that is generally illegal in California) in an effort to avoid paying employment taxes; this places the burden for paying withholding taxes and health insurance squarely on you. There are thousands of highly educated and qualified attorneys competing for the same shrinking pool of jobs, and many are willing to accept less-than-ideal terms in order to remain employed.

Through it all, the student loan debt will remain.

Beyond the Rose-Tinted Glasses

When I was in school, I assumed a pot of gold would be waiting for me upon graduation, but when my turn came, I considered myself lucky just to have a job. It took a few years to start earning a salary that was reasonably commensurate with my ability and experience, and a full six years until my income broke six figures. In the end, the law was indeed a meaningful and challenging career—but those first few years were hard.

I consider myself among the lucky ones.

All schools will paint a rosy picture of your job prospects upon graduation, but employment figures published by the schools do not always tell the full story. While the American Bar Association (ABA) has changed reporting requirements so that employment figures now distinguish between employment in and outside the legal profession, there is no requirement to disclose what those non-legal jobs are. Nor do the employment figures distinguish between those working full-time, those working part-time, and those working gig jobs to make ends meet. The truth is, many lawyers today are not getting a return on their investment in law school.

Many students would not have enrolled in law school had they understood the bleak prospects awaiting them on the passing side of the bar exam. In October 2010, a Boston College 3L wrote an open letter to the Dean asking him to refund two-and-a-half years' tuition. The student had a baby on the way and no job prospects, and he intended to return to teaching. He made a cogent argument that, if his tuition was refunded, the school could be spared the burden of reporting his unemployment to *U.S. News and World Report*, a publication that compiles data and ranks law schools.

Boston College responded with its own open letter, sympathizing with the plight of this student and all law students across the country. The letter highlighted the college's efforts to assist graduates to find employment, and then went on to say, "No institution of higher education can make a guarantee of a job after graduation."

I don't know if this student seriously thought the school would refund him after he'd received five-sixths of a legal education—but if a 3L who put himself through hell for two and a half years is willing to walk away because of weak job prospects, it should serve as a warning to all.

There have been several false advertising lawsuits against schools based upon students' frustrated expectations regarding employment prospects. Thomas Jefferson School of Law, Thomas M. Cooley Law School, and New York Law School, all in the bottom tiers of the rankings, all allegedly misrepresented data regarding their graduates' employment statuses and salaries.

Anna Alburda graduated from Thomas Jefferson in 2008 and took her alma mater to trial. She alleged that, despite incurring $150,000 in student loans (before interest), graduating near the top of her class, passing the bar the first time, and submitting 150 resumes, she only received one job offer. She argued the school misrepresented its post-graduate employment statistics, but a San Diego jury ruled in the school's favor, awarding her nothing, because she declined the single offer she received.

The public's rebuke was unequivocal. Lawyers get no sympathy from society, and suing your school is not a viable Plan B. If you can't find a job despite your good grades and best efforts, you can seek an advanced degree (more debt!), go into business for yourself, or apply your legal acumen to another field entirely.

On that note: I recently received an email from my alma mater promoting a symposium on non-legal careers for law school graduates. When law schools give seminars on job prospects for non-legal careers, you know the job market for lawyers is not good.

It might sound like I'm trying to scare you away from law school—but that's actually not the case. My only objective is to provide an honest picture of the risks and burdens associated with a law education. For many, a *Juris Doctor* degree, coupled with a license to practice law, is a pathway to a very comfortable living. However, the variabilities of the economy and job market can add months or even years to your success journey.

This brings us back to the key point of this chapter: if you want to succeed in law school, you must be willing to walk through a brick wall to become a lawyer. If you're in it just to please your parents, or because you're picturing a glamorous lifestyle like you see in the media, your desire won't see you through these harsh realities.

***

If you've read this whole chapter and can still honestly say, "Heck, yeah, I want to be a lawyer!" then congratulations. You've passed the first test. Law school is, in fact, right for you.

Now, on to the next question:

Are *you* right for law school?

Chapter 2

OVERACHIEVERS WELCOME

IT'S MONDAY MORNING, and I'm up at 6:30 a.m.

I go through my morning routine in preparation for the long day ahead, staring at the handwritten Post-it notes plastered all over my studio apartment, each containing random nuggets of Criminal Law, Real Property, and Torts. I load up my backpack with my casebooks, a three-ring binder containing the case briefs from my Sunday night reading, and some drinks and snacks. The backpack must weigh forty pounds. I also load up a computer bag with my laptop, computer accessories, and any secondary course materials that didn't fit in the backpack. It's the year 2000, so laptops were neither small nor light.

I leave home at 7:30 to arrive on time for my Criminal Law class, which begins at 8:30. I exit the freeway at Front Street in Downtown San Diego, and head north into the Bankers Hill neighborhood. All of the parking near my school campus is metered with a two-hour limit, so after being forced to hunt for parking on hilly streets several blocks away from the school, I've finally sprung for a $65 monthly pass in a parking structure several blocks from campus. I circle to the roof level of the structure before finding one of the few remaining spaces, barely managing to squeeze my SUV into the narrow spot.

I then hike several blocks downhill toward campus with my forty-pound backpack on my shoulders and my twenty-pound computer bag alternating between my left and right hands.

I attend the morning class, then find a quiet cubicle in the library to read case assignments for the following day's classes. Then it's off to the next class, after which I meet friends for lunch. In the afternoon, we kill time in a study room together. We do actually study together, but a chunk of our time is spent fooling around and blowing off steam.

I attend my afternoon class, then settle into another cubicle in the library. We are taught to treat law school as a full-time job, which means, "Don't go home until your work is done." I don't allow myself to leave until my reading and briefing for the next day is complete. I also draft quick summaries of what was discussed in my classes that day.

I then pack my bags and head back to my car in the dark. This time, I'm walking uphill the whole way with my gear. I get home, work out a little, get a bite to eat, watch a little television, then study some more before going to bed well after 10:00 p.m.

This is a day in the life of a law student.

Every day, you'll need to be at your best. Every day, you'll need to give your classes your full attention. It doesn't matter if you're tired, distracted, or just tired of lugging those books around. Law school will consume your life—and you will either develop the skills to thrive in this environment, or you will hate it and burn out.

Which will it be?

Do You Have What It Takes?

You will not start law school at the zenith of your personal or professional development, so don't for a moment think that you need to be great at everything before you walk through the doors.

However, there are certain skills and qualities that are absolutely necessary to achieve success in law school—and that's what we'll be exploring in this chapter.

These skills are:

- Efficiency
- Curiosity
- A strong work ethic
- Attention to detail
- Competitiveness
- Test-taking
- Writing
- Public speaking
- Speed reading

Law school is packed with overachievers. I'd even say that being an overachiever is a prerequisite. To thrive in law school, you have to be the kind of person who is always eager for the next challenge. Of course, we can all burn out if we push ourselves too hard, and in no way am I encouraging that approach. However, if the idea of growing in the areas we'll explore in this chapter doesn't excite you at all—or worse, if you're opposed to growing in these areas—you might not be right for law school.

On the other hand, don't let the above list of optimal skills dissuade you. You don't need to strongly embody all of these before you begin your law school experience; you will have plenty of time to grow, develop, and improve in each area. The key is to discern if these skills excite you and feel attainable.

Let's begin.

ARE YOU EFFICIENT?

As the expression goes, "If you want something done, give it to the busy person."

I thrived under pressure when I was in college, and as a result became very efficient with my time. This skill was critical to my success in law school and later as an attorney.

The pace of law school will make your head spin. The classes are intense, the professors have no tolerance for unprepared students, and your classmates will judge you. It is hard enough to keep up with the daily reading assignments, but you are also expected to brief the cases and outline the material as you go throughout the semester. Most of your time between classes will be spent studying, and your nose will be buried in a book much of the day. You will fall behind and struggle if you can't prioritize assignments, assimilate vast quantities of information, and use your time wisely.

ARE YOU NATURALLY CURIOUS?

While a guest on *Inside the Actor's Studio*, Tom Hanks was asked to name the last career he would ever choose for himself. He responded that he would never be a lawyer "because they do homework for a living."

I found this comment somewhat demoralizing at first, because it's true: lawyers do, in fact, do homework for a living. Before you can answer a client's question or resolve an issue you spot, you will need to research (or have researched in the past) everything to do with the subject. Even when you think you know the answer, the nuance of each situation often requires further research or analysis.

Litigation requires constant research, as legal arguments must be backed up with citations. Every motion requires research and writing a paper. Arguing a motion in court is not unlike taking an exam because you spend hours preparing in advance and must think on your feet at the hearing. Depositions and trials require the same.

What makes this process tolerable—and even enjoyable—is an appreciation for learning. To be a successful litigator, you must be a naturally curious person who enjoys learning, spotting issues, asking questions, performing research, and uncovering the truth.

Depending on your chosen specialty, the profession can expose you to many practice areas such as probate, real estate, construction defect, employment, securities, personal injury, corporate, etc. You might work in several fields or practice areas throughout your career. You will need to learn about the always-evolving law, which requires research. You will also need to take continuing education courses to maintain your license.

In addition to the law itself, you also must learn the real-life, non-legal aspects of each case—otherwise known as *facts*. Your job is to apply the law to the facts. In law school, the facts are spoon-fed to you. As a real-world litigator, you must develop the facts yourself during a phase called "discovery." To effectively identify the questions and areas of inquiry that will further your case, you must be naturally curious and also willing to revise your perceptions and opinions based on new facts that emerge.

For example, if you are litigating a construction defect

case, you must know, or be willing to learn, the basics of construction. Young attorneys are often sent to site inspections in construction cases; this is an opportunity to walk a site (usually a series of homes or an office building) and pick the brains of your expert witnesses. If you are not asking questions of your experts and learning about construction, you're not doing your job, and will not be an effective advocate. I have never worked a day of construction in my life, but from my experience in litigation, I have gained a rudimentary understanding of the roles of the various construction trades and the sequencing of construction projects. This helps me ask better questions and identify where I still have more to learn.

In insurance coverage litigation, you must understand how policies are marketed, underwritten, and sold; the anatomy of the policy itself; and claims handling procedures. In one coverage case, I attended the inspection of the smoldering ruin of a 12,000-square-foot mansion two days after a massive fire. I learned about fire causation while shadowing our retained fire inspector. While we were there, a fire truck unexpectedly showed up. It was the crew that was first on the scene at the fire, and they walked us through the debris to retrace their steps and describe the destruction they witnessed. It was fascinating.

In real estate litigation, you must understand purchase and loan documents and the duties of buyers, sellers, escrows, and lenders.

A medical malpractice or personal injury lawyer should feel like a medical student and know how to perform medical research.

A business attorney should be constantly learning about their clients' trades, professions, or industries, as well as about accounting and tax concepts.

In summary, you will have to learn about the facts of your

case, in addition to the relevant law. You will become intimately familiar with each client's life and/or business, whether the matter at hand involves criminal, civil, or family law. Much of this knowledge will stay with you long after the case is closed; over time, you will become someone who knows a little about many things. For the naturally curious, this is a benefit in and of itself.

But there's more.

At any deposition, you will rely upon detailed outlines, but you will have to carefully listen to the testimony and be prepared to respond with improvised questions, which are rooted in curiosity. The best testimony occurs during free-flowing conversation with a witness while maintaining eye contact (looking at the witness, not your notes). You must be inquisitive and attentive enough to follow up with the testimony and pursue every piece of information and avenue of inquiry that potentially helps your case. You also must sort through information that is harmful to your case, as bad facts are worse when they are unknown.

So, if you do not enjoy learning, doing your homework, and actively listening to others, the practice of law is not for you. Tom Hanks grasped the heart of the profession (likely from working with his own counsel): you will, indeed, be doing homework for a living. The more you enjoy the homework—doing research, finding answers, and building a coherent argument or strategy—the more you'll thrive in the profession.

DO YOU HAVE A STRONG WORK ETHIC?

I took a music theory course as a college freshman. We had pianos for desks, and I played a couple of songs on the piano for my final exam.

I struggled with music theory and reading music. However, I had prior experience playing guitar, so learning a new instrument was intuitive. In my freshman year, I was more interested in partying than studying, and I got an F on the Music mid-term. Fortunately, half the course grade was based on my ability to play the piano, and I did apply myself in that respect. I earned a B for the course on my play alone. If I had applied myself more to the theory and less to the keg parties, that grade could have easily been an A.

If you've made it through college and still have the desire to attend law school and become a lawyer, I'll assume you already have a strong work ethic. But, just in case you managed to somehow pull through on natural talent or sheer luck, I'll lay this down here.

Like the practice of law itself, law school is a speed train. It will not wait for you to catch up if you fall behind. It will not take pity on you when you miss classes or assignments, even if it's for a good reason. You will not get by solely on intuition, common sense, smarts (although those are essential), or luck. You certainly won't be able to balance out utter failures with a few shining moments.

You can't fake it in law school. The only way to succeed is to do the work, and do it *effectively*.

You will have to read and brief hundreds of cases, show up and pay attention in class, prepare your own outlines for each course (borrowing others' outlines is useless), and take every practice exam you can find. Law school conditions you to a new way of thinking because you actually have to *teach yourself the law*. Neither the professors nor the casebooks will teach you directly. You must assemble the puzzle yourself. The professor's job is to teach you to spot the issues and think like a lawyer.

If you are going to keep up in law school and maintain your sanity, you must be a self-starter. More, you must *enjoy* hard work; it has to fill you with a sense of satisfaction and fulfillment. This is true for any career path. If you approach law school like I did my freshman music theory course, you will be wasting your time and money.

DO YOU LOVE DETAILS?

Attention to detail is one of the most important skills a lawyer can have. An effective litigator is someone with the patience and concentration to spend time acquiring, reading, and analyzing case files from multiple angles. Seemingly innocuous documents can yield surprisingly helpful information if you pay attention. Columns of numbers might appear meaningless until you get a calculator and play around.

I once represented the San Diego Zoo in a wrongful termination case. Soon before the plaintiff was fired, she was also working a part-time job at The Home Depot. I subpoenaed her personnel file from The Home Depot and carefully reviewed her job application. (Remember, you must develop the facts yourself.) The handwriting was difficult to read, but she identified an *ex*-employee as her current supervisor at the zoo. She lied about the identity of her supervisor to avoid a negative reference. The application also asked the number of lost workdays that year, and she stated six. I knew from her personnel file that she actually missed closer to twenty days. These discrepancies could have been easily overlooked if I wasn't paying attention, or if I hadn't bothered to issue the subpoena. Instead, I was able to use them to attack our opponent's credibility and improve my client's position.

In another case, my developer client sued an insurance

broker for negligently procuring the wrong kind of coverage. The sole focus in the case was whether my client knew what kind of coverage he was getting and whether the broker made the proper disclosures. The case came down to a credibility battle. The carrier submitted a premium quote to the broker, and the broker created her own form to transmit the quote to my client. From pure curiosity, I put the two quotes side by side to compare the numbers. Sure enough, the premium stated by the carrier was lower than the premium stated by the broker. The broker also padded the quote with meaningless nuisance fees unrelated to any task or service. The broker could not explain the purpose or utility of these fees at her deposition. So, not only did the broker procure useless coverage for my client, but she stole from him! Other attorneys involved in the file were focused solely on the coverage issue, so the fraud and theft had thus far been overlooked.

At the broker's deposition, neither she nor her attorney saw it coming. It was fun to watch my opponent squirm in her chair as she justified fudging the numbers, while her attorney fumbled with documents he previously did not bother to review.

These are just a couple of examples of the many cases I've been involved with personally where tiny details made all the difference. My point here is not to brag about my litigation accomplishments, but rather to underscore the importance of paying attention to detail. You *must* be willing to spend time carefully researching and reading your files, looking at the case from different angles, and exploring novel theories, even if they go nowhere. If you aren't paying attention to the details, you will miss critical facts that could help make your client's case.

In law school, the facts are spoon-fed to you, but your professors will grill you on the nuances of fact patterns and make you analyze the law to the facts in front of the entire class. You'll need to read some cases repeatedly to understand them; however, you can't get bogged down in minutiae. So, it's important to balance your attention to detail with your ability to read quickly, summarize the facts, and identify the issues—while, at the same time, not losing the forest for the trees.

DO YOU HAVE A COMPETITIVE STREAK?

Competitive people see activities as more fun when there's a winner.

Good candidates for law school don't just tolerate competition; they thrive on it, and even love it. Law school grades are given on a strict and unforgiving bell curve. It is not about how well you perform on your own; it's about how you perform compared to everybody else. You will be assigned a rank at the end of your first semester (e.g., twenty-six out of 242). Whenever you speak in class, your professor and classmates will judge and deconstruct everything you say. I've done it, I've seen it, and I've received it. This competitive, cutthroat atmosphere is no place for the timid.

Outside of law school, the practice of law is inherently competitive—particularly in litigation. Most cases involve a winner and a loser (or varying shades thereof). The law even has a system for determining the "prevailing party" when the outcome of a lawsuit renders the "winner" unclear. Judges must grant or deny every motion submitted to them; one side wins, and one side loses. (A motion is a written request that the court does something, such as order responses to discovery, change the scheduling, or dismiss the case.)

In many motions, such as discovery disputes, consequences can be severe because attorney's fees are granted to the prevailing party. Cases can be won or lost in motions. I love motion practice because this is where the action occurs in civil litigation. I used to enjoy honing my skills against senior, more experienced lawyers who would make condescending comments like, "I have shoes/ties older than you." (I've since gotten enough salt in my beard that this doesn't happen anymore.)

Competition is even present within law firms, as associates compete for the managing partner's favor, for lucrative cases, for case assignments, and for the most billable hours. Sometimes, the staff are even more cutthroat than the lawyers!

If you want to succeed in law school, and later in practice, you'll need to nurture your competitive streak. You will have a nagging voice in your head saying, "So-and-so will get the upper hand if I put this book down, so I need to keep going." A competitive drive will make you work harder and realize your full potential because it fuels the necessary fire to succeed. If you don't have that fire, you will have a crisis of motivation when times get tough.

I've seen the impact of a lack of competitive fire firsthand in practice. One of my former coworkers was a very smart guy with over ten years of experience. His problem was that he didn't really care about his work; he was just collecting a paycheck. This lack of motivation showed in his work product, the results of his cases, and in client complaints. He was in the wrong line of work for his personality, and he knew it—but he felt like he'd invested too much time in the legal profession to start over, and he had a family to support. He has since found a niche practice area that better suits his personality, and he supplements his income by doing personal training.

As I learned from Tony Robbins, "Success without fulfillment is the ultimate failure." If you're fulfilled by going above and beyond, law school will bring out your highest potential.

Having spilled ink extolling the virtues of competitiveness, I will also say that there should be healthy limits. While law students are, for the most part, inherently competitive people, don't be a jerk. If someone flubs a question in class or performs below you on an exam, course grade, or class rank, show some humility and grace. All participants benefit when competitiveness is *encouraging, positive, and respectful.* If someone is disappointed with their grade, and you're tempted to show your superior grade, keep in mind that that person is doing the best they can under the circumstances. While we all face the same challenges in the law school curriculum, at the same time, we're all fighting our own battles and struggling with our own distinct blocks and weaknesses. Always be kind and compassionate. This will serve you well in practice and in life, not just in school. There is no reason why competitiveness cannot be positive and encouraging, and if you're not seeing that around you, be the change and model it yourself. Your classmates will respect the hell out of you for it, and since you're going to know some or many of these people later in your career, seeding goodwill in school is always a smart move.

CAN YOU HANDLE STANDARDIZED TESTS?

You endured the SAT before college. You must endure the LSAT before law school. You will endure countless exams during law school, and entire course grades can hinge on just the mid-term and final. Then, of course, you must endure (and pass) the bar exam before getting your law license. To make it through this gauntlet, you will need to become an expert—or at least highly competent—at taking standardized tests.

I don't mean to suggest that someone unskilled at standardized testing has no potential as a lawyer. Far from it. I overcame a terrible LSAT score to become a successful student—and, much later, a seasoned attorney with a thriving practice. However, studying by itself isn't enough. It doesn't matter how well you learn the material, how well you spot issues, or how well you analyze. You won't make it in law school—or even make it *into* law school—if you wilt, freeze, or break down under the stress of standardized tests and exams. A classmate of mine who took the bar in another state reported to me that a nearby test-taker broke down crying during the Multistate Bar Exam (this is a standardized all-day multiple-choice exam required in every state). Can you imagine trying to focus on the bar exam while someone sobs nearby?

On the other hand, if you can learn to produce your best work under pressure—especially time pressure—then you will possess a necessary and critical skill for success both in law school and in the practice of law.

DO YOU WRITE WELL?

During orientation at California Western School of Law, in a legal writing workshop, Professor Barbara Cox told my class, "You are beginning your careers as 'writers.'"

This was a strange comment to us newbies, since television had taught us the legal profession was action-packed and that we would spend our days in the courtroom, going from one trial to another.

In reality, trials are rare—but almost everything a lawyer does involves writing. Here are some examples:

Whenever a legal issue arises, you will have to research and write an objective memo. This will allow you or your boss to evaluate the case, frame the litigation strategy, and advise the client.

In order to file a lawsuit, you will have to draft a complaint. This is the document that alleges the relevant facts and legal theories. If the complaint is poorly pled (for example, if the statement of facts is unclear, or legal elements are missing), your adversary will bring a motion to dismiss, driving up the expense of litigation and eroding your credibility with the court and your own client.

If you want the court to impose any kind of order, you must draft and file a motion. Motions can take many forms, including motions to dismiss, motions to compel responses to discovery, and even mundane motions to change the case scheduling. Every motion requires persuasive writing. Most judges make their decisions based on briefs before oral argument even occurs. Many judges rule solely on the papers without allowing any oral argument.

If a party disagrees with the court's ruling, you'll be drafting appellate briefs before the court of appeal.

You will be constantly writing letters to your adversaries and opposing parties, your clients, insurance companies, and others.

When you settle a case, you will have to draft a settlement agreement. Poorly worded clauses can have real and devastating consequences for your clients.

As you can see, when lawyers aren't doing homework (aka, researching), they're writing. Good lawyers are good writers.

I have encountered several adversaries who were *terrible* writers. They couldn't articulate their point, they confused concepts, their formatting was ugly, they misspelled words, their grammar was poor, they didn't know where to put their apostrophes, and they didn't use correct case citations. When opposing counsel is a poor writer, I grin like a shark smelling blood in the water, because I know I'll look better and more professional during motion practice no matter what. Poor writing will damage my opponent's credibility with the court—an automatic point in my favor. This is simple psychology; it's hard to persuade a judge who lacks confidence in your abilities. (Are you one of those people who loses interest in a book or article upon encountering misspelled words or a poorly written paragraph? Assume the reader of your writing—the judge—is the same way.)

On the other hand, my job can actually be *harder* when opposing counsel is a poor writer, because it's more difficult to oppose an unintelligible brief. This wastes clients' time and money on *both* sides.

My point: Even if your motion is factually, procedurally, and legally correct, you will hurt your case if you write poorly. You need to articulate your points clearly and concisely, and do so in a way that every other professional who reads your work can understand. A college professor once told my class to "always assume that the reader of your work is moody and mean." You, too, should keep this presumption in mind while you write.

Law professors are (usually) more forgiving than judges about bad writing, as essay exams are written under extreme time pressure with little time to proofread, and professors focus more on substance than form. Poor grammar, punctuation, and syntax are often forgiven as long as you're hitting the issues on the professor's grading sheet, because you're being evaluated on your ability to spot and analyze the issues and to correctly recite the law. Your prose and ability to persuade are much less important because there is no "winner," and no rulings are issued. However, if you can provide your professors with the substance they're looking for *and* you can do it cogently, concisely, clearly, and persuasively, your essay will stand out from the rest. Great writing skills coupled with knowledge of the material are how you ace essay exams—and, in some courses, essays dictate 100 percent of your grade.

Also, it's important not to get in the habit of writing sloppily in school, because you will eventually have to persuade prospective employers with your writing. Your resume and cover letter will get you the interview, but employers will almost always request writing samples. If you're looking for a job as a law student or young lawyer, law school writing samples may be all you have, so you should write everything as though it will be seen by a prospective employer.

As you can see, writing skill is an enormous factor in any legal career. So, if you dislike writing, or if you really struggle with writing, you may want to reconsider whether law school and the legal profession are for you. While you'll always be growing and improving as a writer during your career (I'm no exception), you should have some basic writing proficiency by the time you graduate from college.

CAN YOU COPE WITH PUBLIC SPEAKING?

In the classic film *The Paper Chase*, Professor Kingsfield called on the protagonist on the first day of Contracts, mockingly inviting him to "fill this room with your *intelligence!*"[(1)] Law school resembles boot camp in that you are broken down and rebuilt intellectually. Getting called on in class is so intimidating that it can resemble an out-of-body experience.

---

(1) This book contains several references to *The Paper Chase*. To me, this film captures the essence of what it feels like to be a law student and the law school experience (at least at Harvard in the 1970s).

To survive law school, you will need to stare down intimidating professors, maintain your focus under scrutiny, and answer tough questions while the entire class watches (and judges you). Anyone can conjure a smart idea in a library cubicle, but can you do the same while being grilled in front of 100 or more classmates, or in a crowded courtroom? This pressure is a good thing because it prepares you for what you will encounter in your legal career. A professor who coddles students does them no favors. (That said, some professors are unnecessarily cruel, and you will need to weather that, too.)

Your legal career will provide plenty of tense moments with clients, supervising attorneys, opposing counsel, opposing parties, judges, experts, witnesses, and even coworkers. You must be able to stand your ground, look the person in the eye, answer their questions, respond to their arguments, and politely tell them why your position is correct.

I have been stared down and barked at by professors and judges in crowded classrooms and courtrooms, and have had to develop thick skin to manage the stress. I've also had heated exchanges on the record during depositions, in front of my client and the court reporter. I've learned never to take things personally. As a pre-law student, you might not be there yet, and that's okay. However, you will need to be *willing* to grow into a person who can manage their emotions and stay cool under pressure.

The first couple of times you get called on in law school, you might feel your heart rate spike. Your face could get numb. You might have trouble recalling your own name, much less the case you're being examined about. It's okay if this happens. It happens to most people, and it isn't the end of the world. Don't expect perfection from yourself, just commit to improvement over time. Even star quarterbacks throw the occasional pick-six. If you fall on your face when you get called on, don't dwell on it. Develop a sense of humor, never take yourself too seriously, recognize that you have room for improvement, and do what it takes to facilitate that improvement.

Sometimes, an unconventional approach to practice can be helpful. When I was a young lawyer living in Pacific Beach (a beachside party town north of Downtown San Diego), I often played guitar with my next-door neighbor at the open mic night at a local bar. Even on Tuesday nights, the bar was always packed with a couple hundred people. I totally psyched myself out before each set. Would I remember the lyrics and chord structure? Was my guitar in tune? How did we arrange the song? Getting up on stage and greeting the crowd really got the adrenaline going. However, the moment I strummed the first chord, I forgot all about my nerves and just focused on the song. Our allotted fifteen minutes vanished in what felt like sixty seconds. No matter how nervous I was, focusing on the task at hand helped me get over my nerves. I began to treat my law school speaking experiences in the same way. As long as I was prepared, I could relax into the moment—even with classmates and professors circling like piranhas in the water.

Arguing in court, especially in a crowded courtroom on a contested motion, feels eerily similar. Whenever I have a court appearance, whether it's a routine status conference or a motion for summary judgment, I feel nervous to varying degrees. However, just like performing on stage, by the time I state my appearance on the record and address the court, the nerves melt away, and I become totally focused on my job.

Public speaking gets easier with time and practice. You will always remember the first time you were called on in law school, but you will learn to relax. You can also choose your professional path based on how much public speaking you actually want to do. I have friends and acquaintances who are highly successful transactional, governmental, and corporate attorneys (meaning, they draft contracts and negotiate deals rather than litigate cases), and the thought of arguing in court makes them hyperventilate. They still occasionally have to address groups of people in boardrooms or at conferences, so even they aren't off the hook when it comes to public speaking, but their chosen path means they do a lot less of it than others.

We all have bad days. Even the most experienced lawyers get tripped up, tongue-tied, and nervous. We are human, after all! However, if you absolutely hate the thought of public speaking in any situation, even in front of your classmates, law school might not be the right choice for you.

ARE YOU A SPEED READER?

When I say "speed reading," I'm not referring to the practice in any defined or formal sense, nor am I saying that you need to take a course on the topic. However, you will need to become a "speedy" reader to succeed in law school.

The volume of cases you'll need to read in every course will be immense. You'll also be reading secondary course materials, like workbooks, practice exams, and treatises. As such, you must develop the critical skill set of not only quickly skimming the material, but also spotting the issues, identifying the salient facts, and performing legal analysis if you want to keep up with the material.

Some of us are faster readers than others, and I do not judge anyone. If you have a learning challenge, your school might provide you with additional time for some exams and assignments. However, you'll still need to read the course material to make it to exams. Also, once you pass the bar, you'll need to keep up with your workload as an attorney, and you won't get any accommodations there.

If you can quickly read a paragraph/page/chapter/case and retain the material long enough to answer questions under time constraints, then you'll have an advantage in law school. If that's not possible for you now, spend the time to develop that skill set.

***

Regardless of your current strengths, talents, or weaknesses in the above areas, it's not my role, nor am I qualified, to dissuade you (or anyone) from attending law school. If a school accepts your application and offers you a seat, that school's admissions department has already determined that you are, in fact, qualified.

However, if you read any of the above sections and thought, "That's not the kind of person I am," you have a decision to make, because law school may not be the right path for you.

The point of this chapter is to discuss traits that I believe, based on my experience, will give you the greatest chance of success in law school. If you read this chapter and decided law school isn't for you, great! I'll have saved you a lot more money than you spent on this book, plus a year or more of unpleasant educational experience. On the other hand, if you read this chapter and decided that you're an ideal specimen for a law student, that's great, too! You can work to further hone the skills we've discussed and go into your 1L year confident and excited for the challenge ahead. Maybe some of your self-doubt might melt away, too.

Either way, I've done my job.

Part II

Chapter 3

PREPARATION AND POSITIONING

ONCE YOU DECIDE to apply to law school (or if you're just keeping your options open) there are some important steps ahead that you should know about, including your chosen college courses, the LSAT, letters of recommendation, and more. In this chapter, we'll examine all the pieces on the chessboard and discuss how you can optimize each to make your application process as streamlined as possible.

No Particular Major Required

There is no such thing as a "pre-law" major in college. Therefore, theoretically, you may pursue whatever major appeals to you. However, you will be best served by selecting a major that cultivates analytical and critical thinking, research, and writing.

I entered college without a declared major, having no idea what I wanted to do with my life. I took a Critical Thinking course my first semester and was energized by subject matter that actually challenged me to *think*, rather than simply memorize (a sharp contrast to my high school experience). Critical Thinking was an entry-level course within the Philosophy major, and the course list sucked me in with curious-sounding names like Epistemology and Metaphysics. I was hooked.

I double-majored in Philosophy and Communications Studies, mostly due to my natural competitiveness. When I was at junior year orientation, a group of seniors spoke to the incoming freshman class. One guy shared that he was a double major in Kinesiology and Biology. That subject matter did nothing for me, but I recall hearing murmurs around the room when he announced two areas of study. That spoke to the overachiever inside me, whom I had not yet met. That brief moment inspired me to go above and beyond with my coursework.

I knew Philosophy was a natural springboard for law, but I had no plans to become a lawyer at the time, and I declared the major simply because the curriculum was interesting. I recommend that you do the same. Just pick a major that sparks your interest and passion. You'll excel in your studies and grow more from the material when you actually enjoy the subject matter. Hopefully, your major actually interests you, too; it's difficult to make decent grades when you don't care about the subject matter.

If you're reading this as a junior or senior in college and have already declared your major, not to worry. Just about any major, from English to Business to Political Science and even STEM, can provide important and necessary skills and background for a law student. Moreover, your current major may eventually inform your pathway within the field of law. That said, I would suggest taking at least a course or two in the realm of Philosophy.

Philosophy is an excellent choice for pre-law students because it teaches you how to analyze and defend a position—both of which are fundamental lawyering skills. Also, most Philosophy courses are presented according to the Socratic method. Aristotle's writings show that Socrates never taught directly; he taught by asking questions. The lesson would then be revealed through his students' responses and the resulting discussion. Law school is generally taught this way, as the professors teach by asking questions. The transition to law school for a Philosophy major is smoother than for other students because we're already wired to learn this way and are familiar with being publicly put on the spot and interrogated.

While Philosophy may be a good choice overall, any major that cultivates analytical skills and writing will be beneficial. (By this, I mean subject matter that challenges you to compare different schools of thought and adopt and defend a position.) Many majors also offer law-related courses. For example, Communications departments offer Media Law, Business departments offer Business Law, and Philosophy departments offer Philosophy of Law. I took Media Law in college; it was a great primer on defamation, libel, and freedom of speech. I later encountered this material in Torts and Constitutional Law in law school, and some prior schooling on the matter did not hurt.

If your university offers law-related courses, especially if they're within your major, you would be well-advised to take them. These courses look attractive to law school admissions departments, especially when accompanied by an "A."

One final note: I must disagree with the film *Legally Blonde*. Fashion is not a great major for a law student (although, clearly, you'll learn to defend and market your personal aesthetic).

Every Grade Counts

I don't recall the source of this belief, but I had an attitude as a college freshman that first-year grades didn't count, and that performance within my major was the only thing that mattered.

I'm certain this mindset was the product of thoughtful and informed discussions in the keg line—because boy was I wrong.

I prioritized partying and socializing over grades in my freshman year, and it took me a few semesters to straighten out. I found myself at a junior college for a semester as a sophomore, and my GPA took a major hit as a result of my lack of focus.

When I started thinking about post-graduate plans, I learned that first-year grades *do* count. Law schools look at your overall GPA as well as individual course grades. If you have straight A's within your major but the rest of your grades drag your GPA down to a 2.8, top-tier law schools will not find you attractive.

At the end of my sophomore year, I had several Cs on my record and a D in math. After declaring the double major, I became a well of motivation and work ethic and started earning straight A's—but the grades from my first two years pulled down my GPA like an anchor. By my fifth year in college, I had so many units under my belt that my grades became diluted, but I definitely paid the price for not applying myself in those first two years. If I'd worked half as hard in my first two years as I did in my last three, I would have had many more options for law school.

In the latter half of college, I developed a technique for acing my classes. Every professor is looking for something in particular. You will be successful if you can learn how each of your professors calculates your grade. Just focus your energy on executing every task that impacts your grade, play each professor's game, and you will succeed. Remember, every grade on your transcript counts, so don't blow off a class just because it's not in your major or because you don't like the professor. (You'll dislike plenty of professors in law school, and plenty of your colleagues in the legal profession. You'll still have to work with them.)

Letters of Recommendation

All law schools require letters of recommendation in the application process. They want to hear from people who personally know you and can attest to your capabilities. To this end, you are well-advised to nurture positive relationships with your professors and employers, as letters from neighbors, friends, and parents will carry far less weight with admissions.

In my sparsely-populated Philosophy major (I was one of only twelve students), I was fortunate to have Professor Philip Clayton for six classes. As a result, Professor Clayton was intimately familiar with my writing and analytical style, and happily agreed to write a letter of recommendation. You likely attended a school with a higher population than Sonoma State University, and your major courses might have more than twelve people in them, so nurturing relationships could be more of a challenge. If this is the case, make it a point to visit your favorite professors during their office hours and/or interact with the professors during class—but don't become a brown-noser, either. The important thing is that your professors are familiar enough with you that they can write a sincere and informed letter on your behalf.

Another option is to get a letter from your employer. I worked as a kitchen manager during college at a local brew pub, Third Street Aleworks, and became friends with the owner, Todd. One might think working in a restaurant does little to prepare someone for law school, but Todd recognized that running a busy kitchen on a Friday night, multitasking seventeen things at once, supervising the line cooks, and remaining composed when a waitress drops a well-done steak on the ground, are all indicative of a person who can handle the stresses of law school and practicing law. His letter of recommendation said I was "no shrinking violet." I now know from experience that you definitely cannot be a shrinking violet when facing down a professor, opposing counsel, or a cranky judge.

The moral of the story is that unlikely people might recognize qualities you take for granted or do not perceive about yourself, and these qualities might speak volumes about your ability to succeed in law school. The better these people know you, the more effectively they can advocate on your behalf.

Before you start applying to schools, make a list of potential references—people who could write letters on your behalf. If you have cultivated relationships with the right people, they will be flattered that you asked and would be happy to help.

Law School Admissions Test (LSAT)

The two critical factors for law school admissions are your GPA and LSAT scores.

No matter which law schools you're applying to, admissions departments will primarily be concerned with your GPA and LSAT; all the subjective considerations are secondary.

The LSAT is a standardized exam that tests your reading comprehension and your logical and analytical capabilities. There is also an essay section; this does not count toward your score, but rather gives the admissions department something to compare to your "personal statement" in the school application (to ensure you really wrote it).

The LSAT can make your aspirations become reality—or it can force you to seriously reevaluate your goals. Scores range from 120 to 180; anything above 160 should generally get you into a good school (depending, of course, on your GPA). Some people are freaks of nature who sit for the LSAT once without any practice and score a 165. Other people (including yours truly) take all the courses they can find, plus several practice exams, and come nowhere near that score. No matter how smart you are (or think you are), I do not recommend going in cold. The LSAT is an extreme exercise in mental gymnastics, and just like you wouldn't run a marathon without training your body, you shouldn't sit for the LSAT without practice tests. Have a training mentality.

While preparing for the LSAT, I did my best to impose test-like conditions upon myself. My practice scores were average at first, but they steadily climbed as the real thing crept closer. I entered the exam room full of confidence and felt just as confident coming out. Other people were crying outside the exam room, and I took this as an omen that my confidence would translate into a good score. But, when my score arrived in the mail months later—*after* I applied to nine schools—I opened the envelope to discover I'd scored a devastating 148, around the fortieth percentile.

While it might be a huge factor in the admissions process, I do not believe the LSAT necessarily dictates your ultimate success in law school or in the profession. Despite my low score, I graduated law school in the top nineteenth percentile of my class. I'm living proof that if you can at least get *accepted* into a law school after a poor LSAT score, you can still *succeed* in law school. Once you have a seat in the classroom, you're on a level playing field with your peers.

The Personal Statement

Every law school application has a section called the "personal statement." This is an opportunity for you to demonstrate your writing ability and show your humanity behind the LSAT score and GPA.

Schools want to know about your qualifications and aspirations because this gives them an opportunity to evaluate your potential for success. Between students with similar composite scores, a well-composed personal statement could tip the scale in your favor.

Admissions committees read thousands of applications and personal statements yearly, so yours must stand out from the rest. Put yourself in the shoes of the reader. You're staring at a tall stack of applications and need to read fifty more before you can break for lunch. If an essay is putting you to sleep, or if it's poorly written, you're going to manage a couple of paragraphs at most before you put it in the "reject" pile.

You need to come across as witty and intelligent, someone who would make the student body more interesting. This is a tall order for an essay, so don't take this task lightly.

I filled my own personal statements with naïve and idealistic drivel about how I was going to save the world from every scourge imaginable—about how I would be a crusader for justice, pursuing environmental polluters while simultaneously enforcing the first amendment rights of underdog media outlets. I was going to be Superman with a bar card.

As I've already confessed, I didn't get admitted to many schools. Re-reading those essays from my current perspective makes me cringe.

After a year at California Western, I needed to complete a fresh application for the University of San Diego. My 1L year hardened me and brought me back to earth. I still discussed my aspirations, but I kept it focused. I also shared the study methodology that enabled me to master the material in my 1L curriculum. Obviously, I did better in that second round.

So, go ahead and share how you're going to put away all the bad guys. Just don't promise that you're going to rewrite the Tax Code at the same time. Tell a coherent story about your goals, and how you intend to create success (or notoriety) in your career. Remember, your future success will reflect upon your school—so try to portray yourself as someone who will contribute to the legal profession and therefore the school itself.

Law School Admissions Council

The LSAT is administered by the Law School Admissions Council (LSAC), a non-profit corporation that has existed since 1947. All law schools accredited by the American Bar Association (ABA) are LSAC members.

Every law school applicant must submit their transcripts and letters of recommendation to the LSAC's Credential Assembly Service (CAS). Applicants are required to provide this information to the CAS in advance, and schools receive your information directly from the CAS when you apply. This streamlines the application process so you don't have to waste time (and postage) sending transcripts and letters of recommendation to multiple schools. That said, you will need to direct all undergraduate and post-graduate schools you have attended to send your records to the CAS. The CAS will then combine your transcripts, letters of recommendation, and LSAT score to create your own personal report, which law schools will evaluate in conjunction with your application.

Once you have received your LSAT score, forwarded all your information to the LSAC, and sent in your applications, you can log into your LSAC account and select the schools where you want to send your information. LSAC sends a report to every school you select for a fee (which, at last check, was around $35). This charge is in addition to the one-time LSAC/CAS document assembly fee of $50. These costs, in addition to your school application fees, can easily total over $1,000, so be careful about firing off applications at random.

Take the time to understand the process before you start applying to schools. Visit the LSAC website and familiarize yourself with its procedures as well as the individual application procedures for each of your chosen schools. (You aren't applying to just one school, right?)

The School Selection Process

RANKINGS: IT'S ALL ABOUT THE NUMBERS

Law schools live and die by their ranking.

The most followed and influential ranking system is the *U.S. News & World Report*, which evaluates schools based on a four-tiered system. Of course, the tiered ranking system is not without controversy because its methodology is partly subjective; some say this compromises the journalistic integrity of the publication. Several top-tier law schools, such as Harvard, Yale, Columbia, Stanford, Berkeley, and Georgetown, have withdrawn from the *U.S. News & World Report*, contending that the rankings treat students performing public service work as if they were unemployed, thus skewing the rankings and disincentivizing schools from encouraging public service work.

The top 100 schools in the country comprise the first tier, and the rest are divided between the second through fourth tiers. Law schools are ranked by different weights attributed to the following criteria: Quality Assessment (peer review and lawyer/judge review); Selectivity (median LSAT and undergraduate GPA, acceptance rate); Placement Success (employment of graduates, bar passage rate); and Faculty Resources (expenditures per student, faculty to student ratio, library resources). Schools must be accredited by the ABA in order to be ranked at all.

Rankings increase a school's prestige, which in turn increase demand and drive up tuition.

ACCREDITATION

The American Bar Association (ABA) has an accreditation program for law schools. I won't detail the standards here, but schools must generally demonstrate compliance with the ABA's standards for a "sound legal education." This encompasses several factors, one of the more important being that 75 percent of graduates who sit for the bar exam must pass it within two years. There are about 200 accredited law schools in the U.S.

Non-accredited schools have lower barriers to entry and cost less, but job prospects and bar passage rates are considerably lower. There are about thirty non-accredited law schools in the U.S., and many of them are in California, which is a big market for lawyers.

Recognizing that most students at non-accredited schools struggle to pass the bar exam, and to weed out bar exam-takers who are more likely to fail, the California State Bar requires first-year students to take and pass the "Baby Bar Exam" before they can begin their second year of school.

If you can get accepted to an accredited school, I strongly advise you to attend that school over any unaccredited school. Your diploma will carry more weight and your employment prospects will be much brighter. You will also be more likely to pass the bar exam, and you won't have to sit for the Baby Bar after your first year.

WHERE TO APPLY: SAFETY AND REACH SCHOOLS

You should have a hierarchy in mind about the schools you would like to attend. There are some schools you might kill for an acceptance letter from, and others that inspire ambivalence. I strongly advise you to apply to both "safety" and "reach" schools. This might be controversial, but if you only apply to one school because you *really* want to attend that school, you should evaluate how much you really want to be a lawyer.

Law schools are deluged with thousands of applications every year, and space is limited. While applicants are judged on subjective factors such as their essay, choice of major, extracurricular activities, and letters of recommendation, the composite score of college GPA plus LSAT is the initial gatekeeper. Subjective factors are examined only once an applicant's composite score is within the school's accepted range (which increases the higher a school is ranked).

I hadn't yet taken the LSAT when I began my application process. I figured my subjective strengths, like my double major, senior thesis, and restaurant management experience would be recognized and separate me from the pack despite my pedestrian GPA. Surely, the admissions departments would recognize my abilities and see that I was ready for the challenges of law school. Plus, of course, I would ace the LSAT …

Well, I've already shared how that worked out.

Out of the nine schools I applied to, I was accepted to three and waitlisted by a fourth. None of my "reach" schools—including my top pick, the University of San Diego—were interested. I badly wanted to move back to San Diego, which is why I chose California Western, a lower-ranked school, even though my other two acceptance letters were from slightly more prestigious schools.

I wasn't complaining. I had friends—smart friends—who weren't accepted to *any* law school. I had my foot in the door, and I would make the best of it. And, as I've shared, I was able to transfer to USD after my first year.

I learned the hard way that my many fine subjective qualities were insufficient to get me accepted at top-tier schools. However, if you have a good GPA and LSAT score, your subjective attributes may give you an edge over other applicants, so don't be afraid to lean hard on those aspects on your applications.

Finally, while it's great to get into your top pick school, don't put all your eggs in that basket. Cast a wide net of applications so you have options. You could get accepted to your top pick—but a lower-tier school might offer you a scholarship. The more attractive a candidate you are, the more options you will have.

The most important thing is that you get in *somewhere.* As long as you make the grades, you can always transfer to the school of your choice in your second year. And, even if that plan doesn't work out, you will still have a degree and a law license at the end of the journey. While a prestigious degree may open more doors at first, once you've established yourself in your practice area, no one will really care if you attended School A or School B.

BAR PASSAGE RATE

How well do your prospective schools prepare their students for the rigors of the bar exam?

Bar passage rates are critical because you can't do (or earn) much in the legal profession without a law license. That said, passing the bar is only mandatory if you actually intend to practice law; plenty of people got the degree but not the license and do very well for themselves in other fields.

In addition to the bar passage rate overall, you should know the success rate of each school's first-time test-takers (because you obviously hope to be among them). Also, people taking the exam for a second, third, or fourth time have consecutively lower passage rates. For example, the July 2011 passage rate for California was 54.8 percent. First-time test-takers were 71.9 percent of those being tested, and 69 percent of those first-timers passed the bar. In contrast, only 18 percent of those repeating the exam passed.

Bar passage rates are readily available online. In fact, a web search of "bar passage rates" in your state will lead you to relevant historical data. If your school's bar passage rate for first-time test-takers is favorable compared to the rest of the state, this demonstrates that the school competently prepares its students for the bar exam. This factor should be given considerable weight as you evaluate prospective schools.

The school you choose needs to provide broad exposure to many practice areas. Certain schools are known for specializing in certain subjects, and most emphasize and prioritize subject matter tested on the bar exam. However, not all schools—even those that charge hefty tuition—do a good job helping students pass the bar. For example, in July 2011, Thomas Jefferson School of Law in San Diego posted a dismal California bar passage rate of 33 percent, compared to that year's statewide passage rate of 54.8 percent.

You should also consider each school's bar passage rate over multiple years, always in contrast to statewide passage rates. For example, if the passage rate is very low one year, but the state passage rate is also lower than usual, it might mean that the exam was simply more difficult that year, and that the numbers should be taken in context. What you're really evaluating is how the school's overall passage rates compare to the statewide averages over the course of several years.

If you choose a school with average or below-average bar passage rates (and there might be reasons why you would do this, such as scholarship offers or geographical location), you should be prepared to invest additional funds in bar preparation services. Failing to pass the bar on the first try means another six months of studying, delayed income, financial stress, and deferred student loan payments. Your likelihood of success also falls each time you re-take the exam.

POST-GRADUATE EMPLOYMENT RATES

While researching prospective schools, consider the post-graduate success of the alumni as well as the school's ranking. Unless you're in the minority of students who plan to pursue alternative careers in business or academia, a law degree won't hurt your employment prospects. As you evaluate your school options and consider the financial costs of each, it is helpful to know about your options after you pass the bar.

All schools publish their recent graduates' bar passage rate, employment rate, and median salary for each scholastic year. This is important information you cannot ignore because it speaks volumes about your prospects. At the same time, you should take this information with a grain of salt because, as we explored in earlier chapters, the information provided by law schools can be highly misleading; this can result in disillusionment and disappointment when your results don't conform to your expectations.

Law schools do not directly publish their post-graduate data. Instead, they submit the data to the *U.S. News & World Report* for publication. The *U.S. News & World Report* makes some of this information available online for free, but it locks certain information behind a paywall, so be prepared to fork out $30 or so to get a bigger statistical picture. The reporting standards are governed by the ABA; however, the numbers are unaudited. The schools can state whatever they want—and schools have a financial incentive to fudge the numbers because rankings directly influence enrollment.

This data used to be critically flawed as a rule, as schools did not differentiate at all between the various types of post-graduate employment. Students were reported as "employed" as long as they worked *somewhere*—whether that "somewhere" was a prestigious law firm or the local grocery store. I've heard tales of unscrupulous schools that temporarily employed some graduates part-time for the purpose of improving their employment rate. To state the obvious, this is grossly immoral. Nobody wants to pay $150,000 or more and endure the stress of passing the bar exam just to work for minimum wage at their school's bookstore.

Fortunately, the ABA, which dictates the data law schools must report, has amended its guidelines to require schools to report the nature of graduates' work. Schools now report graduates who were employed for at least a year in positions that either required a bar license or where a *Juris Doctor* degree provided an advantage. This is helpful—but, as you'll see, these numbers can be far from inspiring.

Because I did well in school and had good grades, I assumed there would be pot of gold waiting for me on the other side of graduation. Reality had different plans for me, and also for most of my classmates. The profession has ultimately been rewarding to me, but, as I shared in the introduction, there were several lean years and toxic environments between graduation and my current success. I'm sharing this to help manage your expectations, not to discourage or dissuade. You can have a very lucrative career if you work hard and make good decisions; just don't expect a pot of gold after you graduate.

Location Counts, Too

While rankings, admissions, and bar passage rates are all important metrics for choosing a school, you should also consider location.

When choosing a law school, spend time in the surrounding city or town as well as on campus. Can you envision yourself living there? Can you afford housing in the immediate area—and, if not, will your commute be reasonable? During your (rare) moments of free time, will the area give you access to amenities you enjoy?

Right before my last semester of college began, I visited San Diego and toured the campuses at USD, Cal Western, and Thomas Jefferson. This provided a tremendous wellspring of motivation when I returned to finish my undergraduate studies. I also got to sit in on Real Property classes during my tours, which gave me a feel for what to expect. Seeing the campuses and sitting in live classrooms removed some of my fear of the unknown and replaced it with excitement.

I still recall a particular class about deed recording priority. I had gone surfing that morning and gotten tumbled around by the waves, which resulted in a few tablespoons of ocean water settling into my sinuses (surfers know what I mean). While I was auditing the class, already feeling a bit self-conscious from the curious glances of *real* law students, my nose turned on like a faucet, emptying salt water from my sinuses and onto my desk. Despite my embarrassment, I was beyond excited to be applying to schools in a place where I could surf.

After getting accepted to Cal Western, I found a studio apartment in San Diego's Pacific Beach neighborhood, a college party town close to campus. At first, it seemed ideal—but quickly grew frustrating when I realized I was surrounded by young adults who partied every night of the week. I once missed a morning appointment because a neighbor blocked my car in the shared driveway and was too hungover to hear me pounding on his apartment door the next morning.

Also, you will become sick with boredom and burn out quickly if you confine yourself to the school library and your apartment. Because of my location, I was able to change my routine (and escape the riotous neighborhood) by taking my casebooks and laptop to a variety of parks and beaches in the area. This helped keep me fresh, so I didn't feel like a robot whose only function was to study. If you have the opportunity, you should choose a school in an area where you have access to activities that feed your creativity and wellbeing, and where you can change the scenery easily while still having the shortest possible commute.

A Caution for Scholarship Recipients

Many law students are fortunate enough to receive partial or full-ride scholarships. This is a tremendous opportunity given the cost of tuition, and one you should consider carefully.

If one school offers you a scholarship while another does not, it can be tempting to simply choose the scholarship option. You may need to decide between paying tuition at a top-tier school or attending a lower-tier school for discounted or free tuition. I was not a scholarship candidate, given my grades and LSAT—but if you are so blessed, there are several factors to consider before you jump on that scholarship.

As I stated earlier, the source of your degree will matter far less in a decade than it does in the year after graduation. However, your alma mater will always be referenced on your resume, your online profiles, and the state bar registry. If your choice was, like mine, between attending a fourth-tier school and not going to law school at all, the choice is obvious—go to the school. However, if you have the opportunity to attend a top-ten school and are also offered a full ride at a school with a less impressive reputation, consider whether the opportunities provided at the top-ten school—and perhaps just as importantly, the contacts you make there—could balance out or even exceed the cost of tuition.

If you're thinking, "Well, what if I just did year one for free, and then transferred to a better school later, like you did?" I'll stop you right there. Most scholarships are conditional upon you completing your degree at that school. No school wants to pay for your whole first-year tuition only to have you pack up and transfer as a 2L. While a school can't *prevent* you from transferring, you will be contractually bound to reimburse your tuition if you do so. This is a major incentive to stay put. Tuition reimbursement is designed to make transferring prohibitively expensive.

Also, don't let a scholarship go to your head. Maybe you received it because of exemplary grades and a high LSAT score—or maybe the school just wanted to increase its enrollment in a certain demographic. Even if the school is paying your way, you will be subject to the same curve as everyone else, and you will have to make the cut like everyone else. Proving yourself worthy of a free ride should motivate you to work harder; after all, the school is literally investing in you, hoping you will have an illustrious career and enhance the school's reputation.

Lastly, do not publicize your scholarship to anyone—especially not to your classmates. It's nobody's business how your tuition is paid. Rumors of scholarships move quickly, and people with known scholarships are closely watched by their classmates; when you know someone is on a full ride, it's tempting to measure yourself against them. I knew some scholarship recipients I greatly respected, and others I thought seemed unworthy. That sounds judgmental, but these latter students were often unprepared, became tongue-tied during Socratic questioning, and did not distinguish themselves in the classrooms or in the rankings. I'd be lying if I said that didn't cause resentment.

While the opinions of others are none of your concern, you should expect extra layers of competition and judgment if you don't keep your scholarship to yourself.

In summary, scholarships are a wonderful opportunity to save on tuition costs, and you should inquire into scholarship programs that align with you. If you receive a scholarship, make sure you understand the terms, specifically that you may be required to reimburse tuition if you transfer to another school.

***

Entering the law school application process prepared and knowledgeable about what's to come will increase your chances of acceptance at the right school for you. With the right perspective and tactics, you will set yourself up for a successful application process and navigate the available options with an eye to your long-term success.

Part III

Chapter 4

WELCOME TO LAW SCHOOL

CONGRATULATE YOURSELF for deciding to attend law school, and for investing in the educational process to become a lawyer. To get this far you've at least attained a bachelor's degree and survived the rigors of the LSAT and the application process; you have also hopefully gained some life and work experience. Now, you're either committed to a school and possibly relocating to attend, or you're close to deciding where you'll be attending.

Don't Skip Orientation

Given my sub-par GPA and LSAT score, Cal Western enrolled me in a mandatory pre-orientation program a month before orientation and the real first semester began. The purpose of the program was not to teach us about the law, but about *how* to be a law student. The program was not offered to all incoming 1Ls, and I was required to attend because of my low composite score.

I can honestly say that I owe much of my success in law school to this program. Plus, it didn't hurt to have the chance to make friends before everyone else arrived on campus. I had a group of friends/study partners before the semester even began.

The pre-orientation program included legal writing, how to spot issues, and how to brief cases, but it also provided insight into how attending law school would feel. Our professors conducted our classes as if we were already in law school—including lots of reading assignments—but the intimidation factor was absent. I left that program knowing what would be expected of me as a law student, but also with a comprehensive strategy for studying efficiently and effectively. This enabled me to hit the ground running.

I also participated in Cal Western's orientation program, which further eroded my fear of the unknown. Some would rather spend the weeks before school begins doing as little as possible or spending time with loved ones—but in a competitive atmosphere like law school, you'll need any advantage you can get. So, if your chosen school provides any orientation activities, I highly suggest you participate.

Before school begins, familiarize yourself with the campus, facilities, and administration, as well as the area around the campus. You're going to start stronger if you already know where to park and eat during the school day, and have your books and supplies assembled and ready to go.

Be Smart About Supplies

BOOKS

Your campus will have its own bookstore where you can purchase all required reading and study resources. However, that doesn't mean you should buy everything there, nor that everything you need is there. For example, you might find an independent scholastic bookstore in the area that competes directly with the law school and offers better prices. I personally found a wide variety of study materials at an indie store about ten minutes from campus.

I purchased all my law school materials from brick-and-mortar bookstores, so I cannot speak to the online experience. Still, you can absolutely save money by purchasing your casebooks from reputable online retailers. Just be sure to order them in plenty of time before school begins, since you don't want to walk into your first day of 1L without your books in hand (and without having completed the first reading assignment).

Used books are tempting because they come at a steep discount. However, pay close attention to the book's condition; in particular, try to discern whether the book's previous owner got carried away with the highlighter. You won't be able to confirm the book's condition with online purchases, nor should you necessarily trust that a photo accurately represents the product you will receive. Bookstores generally don't buy used books in poor condition, but online retailers aren't so scrupulous. If another person's scribbling won't distract or derail you, used books can be a great option—but I personally stayed away from them for that reason.

YOUR SUPPLY LIST

Before entering the bookstore (online or in real life), it's wise to plan in advance for what you do and do not need to purchase—not unlike the grocery store.

You will need to pick up the following essentials from bookstore(s) *before* school starts:

- *The assigned casebooks for each course.* There might be multiple casebooks on the same subject matter, so be careful to get books by the correct authors. These are very expensive; you should expect to spend between $80–$250 for each casebook.
- *Separate three-ring binders for each course,* plus plenty of dividers and blank paper. While we all have different learning styles, to really learn this material you should create tangible printed work product. (More on this later.)
- *An ample supply of pens and highlighters.* You will consume an obscene number of highlighters, so you can never have too many. A handful of highlighters will likely only last you a couple of weeks, so be sure to load up and replenish your supply often.
- *Index cards.* 4 x 6" or 5 x 5" will do.
- *A legal dictionary.* (This resource will be discussed in detail in an upcoming chapter.)
- *Secondary course materials.* (Also discussed in detail later.)
- *Durable bags to carry everything.* Casebooks are surprisingly heavy, and you need a strong bag that won't rip under the weight. A hiking backpack or even a rolling briefcase can be helpful.

If you are among the majority of students who choose to use a laptop, you'll need even more gear:

- *A computer bag.* This will need sufficient padding, compartmentalized storage, and a means of securing the computer (such as a Velcro strap that prevents the computer from shifting) so it doesn't get banged around by your books and supplies. As I mentioned in Chapter 2, I used a laptop, and had both a heavy-duty backpack and a leather computer bag, and both were filled to capacity every day. I felt like a burro lugging all that gear around, but I was like a mobile law office. (Of course, laptops are much smaller and lighter today, so I've just dated myself, but you get the picture.) The last thing you want is a cracked or damaged laptop because your gear wasn't properly stored.

- *Storage media.* Do not trust your hard drive or cloud server. If one tiny thing goes wrong, you could lose hundreds of hours of work, or a connection failure could render your files inaccessible. When I was in school, I had a small carrying case for all my floppy disks (yes, dating myself again). Now that technology has evolved, you should consider an external hard drive, zip drive, or other physical backup—something that will allow you to access your files even if you are unable to get online. At the very least, you should save everything to two unique cloud accounts (for example, Google Drive and iCloud) so that if one server is interrupted you will still be able to retrieve your files.
- *A reliable printer and stacks of printer paper.* You will need to print the notes and outlines you spend so much time on; those documents should go in your three-ring binders.
- *A three-ring punch machine* so you can get all those documents into said binders.

I also recommend that you buy the following optional items, although these are more tailored to my personal study habits:

- *Post-it notepads.* From my first year through the bar exam, I wallpapered my apartment with small bits of legal knowledge. I am a visual learner, so this helped me commit difficult concepts to memory. I could literally close my eyes and think of the note on my bathroom mirror, and see my own handwriting in my mind.
- *A metal clasping ring.* I created flashcards for every subject and kept them bound together with a metal ring. (The three-hole punch came in handy here, too.) My flashcards took a beating but the clasping ring held them together.
- *Noise-canceling headphones and a good music selection.* Music or even ambient noise will help you get through those endless hours in the library. There are certain albums I associate with law school, and even twenty-three years later hearing Soundgarden gives me law library flashbacks.
- *A book stand.* I found this gem at the campus bookstore. It's basically a miniature easel that props up a book, notes, or a tablet. Your grandmother may have had one in her kitchen to hold her cookbook. I still occasionally use my law school book stand in practice today. In fact, I used it while editing this book!

SECONDARY MATERIALS

In addition to your required materials, you may also consider secondary materials: non-assigned, "optional" educational materials that track the concepts in your casebooks. Often, these books teach the same concepts as your casebooks, but contain actual discussions about the concepts in an organized manner. Therefore, they can help you synthesize and understand the casebooks. I placed "optional" in quotes because they're mandatory if you want to excel in law school and rank competitively with your classmates. However, if you don't care about such things, skip this step.

Law school bookstores carry secondary materials for just about every course. These books generally take three forms: commercial outlines, hornbooks, and practice exam books.

Commercial Outlines

Commercial outlines are cogent, abbreviated, digestible summaries of a given course. Outlines are amazing educational tools because they help you synthesize the material, showing you what concepts go where and how they interrelate. You must create your own outlines from scratch if you are to have any success in law school, but commercial outlines are an immensely helpful tool because they show how an outline is done.

You are going to outline every course you take.

For example, consider the concept of contract formation in your Contracts course. If you review your commercial Contracts outline at or around the same time your class covers this material, you will receive a valuable alternate perspective. So, read the commercial outlines contemporaneously with your assigned reading. It's extra work, but you'll absorb the concepts much faster, and you'll perform better when you get grilled in class and during exams. I can't count how many times I was stymied by a concept in my casebook or in class, and a commercial outline helped me make sense of the material. Commercial outlines were in my backpack every day.

In summary, commercial outlines are well worth the investment if they are used to supplement the required reading and help you synthesize the material. However, if you are too lazy to make your own outline and think you can learn by simply reading an outline somebody else wrote, commercial outlines will impede your learning and should be avoided.

There are many brands of outlines to choose from. I recommend *Gilbert Law Summaries*, *Examples & Explanations*, and *Emanuel*. These books range in price from $30–$40 apiece, so they will add several hundred dollars to your annual budget, but they are well worth the investment if used properly.

Hornbooks

Hornbooks, or legal treatises, are detailed historical discussions of the law. These books are just as big and heavy as casebooks, if not bigger. Each hornbook is labeled just like your law courses: Torts, Criminal Law, Real Property, etc.

Judicial opinions *are* law, and casebooks are raw republications of judicial opinions. Casebooks seldom come with commentary; you are expected to learn the law by reading the cases. That's how lawyers were trained in the old days, and it isn't much different now. However, while casebooks are composed of about 90 percent written judicial opinions and 10 percent discussion and analysis, hornbooks are the opposite. They don't republish cases verbatim; instead, they summarize and discuss the law, tracking its evolution over time. Hornbooks can read like extremely detailed lectures, often straying into obscure discussions of history, public policy, and philosophy.

As with commercial outlines, hornbooks can be useful as a supplement to the required reading and can shed light on problematic areas. However, after wasting fifty dollars on a Torts hornbook myself to consult it only a couple of times, I am qualified to advise you against *purchasing* any hornbooks. They are too expensive and heavy to carry around, and you won't have enough time to read them in detail. Instead, when necessary, consult a hornbook for free at your school's law library.

Practice Exam Books

Practice exam books are exactly what they sound like. These books are broken down by course material and contain various multiple-choice and essay practice exams.

You can never take too many practice exams. Multiple-choice exams require a healthy mental constitution as well as substantive knowledge, so you will need all the preparation you can get. Exercise those mental muscles often. These books are helpful not only because they contain relevant materials, but because they teach you *how to take exams*, a critical skill in and of itself. The California bar exam (known as the Multistate Bar Exam) has 200 multiple-choice questions.

Additionally, practice exam books don't just churn out correct answers and leave the analysis to you. They explain *why* the right answer is the right answer. The only downside to using them is that you might spin your wheels a bit on irrelevant material and test yourself on material that your professor or casebook omitted for good reason. Despite this, I consider practice exam books a worthwhile investment overall.

One tip: write your answers on separate sheets of paper so you can re-use and re-sell the book.

Your First Year

Once you've completed orientation, gotten familiar with the campus, and purchased your supplies and materials, you'll be as ready as you can be for the semester to begin.

However, there are a few more things to know before you formally become a 1L.

FIRST-YEAR OVERVIEW

For most, law school is a three-year commitment. Many schools also have four-year programs for part-time students. As I've already shared, first-year students are known by the label of "1L"; second-year students are known as "2L" and third-year students are, you guessed it, "3L."

Your first year is guaranteed to be the most intense educational experience of your life, and it can be scary at times. If you can survive the first year—and, even more, if you can *thrive* during this critical period—you will emerge with the belief that there is no challenge you cannot overcome. If you can teach yourself to "think like a lawyer" and devote yourself full-time to learning the law, the analytical wiring in your brain will literally change, and you will become a more critical and organized thinker and writer.

Once you get through the first year, the intensity and pace will slow down significantly. By your third year, you will no longer feel intimidated by your professors or your classmates, and the experience will feel a lot like college.

However, your first year is critical, and you will need to earn the right to call yourself a 2L. Not everyone will make the cut.

Your 1L class will be divided into groups called "sections." Each section will have every class together. By the end of your first year, you will know everybody in your section quite well. These people are your future colleagues; you could end up working alongside some of them, or you might have cases against some of them. I've worked on more than one contentious case against a former classmate. I've also had the opportunity to be co-counsel and work a case with another classmate.

THINKING LIKE A LAWYER

Most of the concepts, at least in your first year, will involve *elements*—the checklist of facts that must be present before a legal concept applies. For example, trespass has the elements of: (1) ownership or a right to possession; (2) intentional entry to land; and (3) damages. All of the elements have to be satisfied before there is a cognizable claim for trespass. The majority of Torts and Criminal Law courses involve the memorization of dozens of torts and crimes and their elements, defenses, exceptions, and policies. You will be presented with convoluted fact patterns and asked to untie the knots by applying the law to the facts. The key to navigating these fact patterns and responding to your professors' Socratic questioning is to spot the issues and analyze the elements of the relevant legal concepts. The analysis is conducted pursuant to a formula described below.

There are two manifestations of the law. The first includes the statutes, regulations, ordinances, and rules that exist at every level of government, from municipalities and counties to state and federal government, and also within state and federal agencies. Statutes are created by legislatures. Regulations and rules are created by rulemaking agencies. Ordinances are created by municipal and county entities.

Because each state has its own penal and civil codes, you will not learn about statutes or state-specific laws in school;

instead, you will learn about the "common law," which is judicially-created law that has evolved over hundreds of years, commencing in England. Common law is the written opinions of judges. As we learned in high school government class, the role of the judge is to interpret the law. When judges interpret the law, their written opinions themselves become law.

All federal and state judges reduce their orders to writing. Appellate orders are often published, becoming precedents for future cases, and lower courts must follow the precedents set by higher courts (known as the doctrine of *stare decisis*). Attorneys have to research these cases, which are cited in briefs and oral arguments. If the case is favorable to you, you will cite it and argue why it is similar to your case and why it should apply; this is called *analogizing*. If the case is not favorable, then you will argue why it is dissimilar and why it should not apply; this is called *distinguishing*. The lawyer's job is to analogize and distinguish the cases to suit each client's situation. Often, the lawyer will have to analogize *and* distinguish within the same case. In addition, the statutes, regulations, ordinances, and rules are interpreted or explained by the case law, so you have to analyze both together.

Citing the law correctly, however, is only part of the challenge. You are expected to use your brain to *analyze*. You have to articulate the legal issue and summarize the relevant law, but the equally critical task is to apply the law to the facts, and this is where the analogizing and distinguishing occurs.

Our legal system employs the "adversarial theorem," where each side zealously advances their version or interpretation of the facts and the law, and the trier of fact, the judge or the jury, is supposed to find the "truth." The theory is that the truth will emerge when two sides zealously present their versions of the facts. Whether or not this system is an adequate means of discovering the truth, or what kind of "truth" emerges, is subject to debate—but that discussion is way beyond the scope of this book.

In law school, it doesn't really matter how you conclude an issue, as long as it halfway makes sense. The process is formulaic: only answer the question asked, identify the legal or factual issue, summarize the *relevant* facts, cite the applicable law, analyze, then conclude. Rinse and repeat. Legal analysis is taught in the IRAC format: Issue, Rule, Analysis, Conclusion. This helps you stay organized while analyzing convoluted fact patterns. This is what I mean by "thinking like a lawyer." Over time, you won't think so rigidly in IRAC terms because it will become second nature.

I regularly encounter attorneys who stray from the IRAC formula in practice, and their writing is a mess. Too often, I see briefs with stream-of-consciousness writing without any structure, aimlessly wandering between factual analysis and legal analysis. When opposing counsel lacks the ability to perform basic legal analysis, you have a competitive advantage, and will be in a position of strength to persuade the judge in your favor.

In my first-semester Legal Skills course, the whole class was given the same fact pattern involving an incident at a backyard BBQ. A man grilling in his backyard became upset at a neighbor and made a menacing gesture. The issue was whether an "assault" occurred. We were each assigned different states and told to research the relevant law in our states so as to analyze the actors' rights and duties. (This happens all the time in actual practice: you will be given a fact pattern by your supervising attorney or by a client, and you will have to research the law to determine your client's rights or liability.) After giving us a few days to research the law in our respective states, the professor asked whether the intimidating neighbor was liable. Students responded by analyzing the nuances of the fact pattern and spotting issues. The professor nodded respectfully and agreed with everything he heard, but he seemed to expect more. One student (who, admittedly, was not me) responded with, "I was assigned to Texas, and in that state the cases hold that ..." That was what the professor was looking for. Legal analysis has to start with the *law*; it is the skeleton of your analysis. The analysis begins only after the law has been summarized.

As you enter this new world of analytical thinking and analysis, remember this: what *you* think about the facts in the abstract doesn't matter, because facts are meaningless unless applied to the law. In the above example, we (the students) committed the cardinal sin of analyzing the facts in a vacuum without any reference to the law. Lawyers must identify the Issue, state the applicable Rule, Analyze the facts to the law, then Conclude.

To summarize: The IRAC method provides the building blocks for thinking like a lawyer. Law school teaches you how to think like a lawyer. But in the end, you will have to teach the law to yourself.

BE READY TO GO ON THE FIRST DAY

Remember during college when the first day of each class was all about what the class would teach you, but you were too busy people-watching your new classmates to care?

Well, don't expect that kind of grace period. The first day of law school actually starts with the law, and the Socratic method begins immediately. I found that some professors ratcheted up their intensity at the beginning of the semester to get a feel for who could hold up under the pressure, then mellowed out as the semester progressed.

By the time you set foot in your classroom on day one, you will be expected to have purchased the course materials and done the required reading. (Yes, reading assignments will be posted *before* the first class, and you should ready yourself to be called on that day.) On my first day in the Real Property class, our professor called on a student who had no idea there was a reading assignment. The professor was far from pleased. I still remember the student's face because I was so embarrassed for him. My Real Property professor was the same one I had in the pre-orientation program, so I knew better than to walk into his class unprepared.

Don't be remembered as "the one who didn't do the reading." If you're in any way unsure of what is required of you to prepare for day one, do the work to find out. Law school doesn't gently build to a crescendo; it begins at breakneck speed and maintains the pace throughout. You need every advantage you can get as a new law student, and you will do yourself a terrible and unnecessary disservice by starting out behind.

NO PARTICIPATION TROPHIES

On day one, look to the person on your left, then the person on your right. One of you won't be here next year.

Law schools literally cull their herds of students. Some schools will fail up to a third or more of their first-year class. Those students must then choose between repeating the entire first-year curriculum or calling it quits. I saw this happen to many outgoing, driven, and bright students; to a class president; to a good friend of mine; and even to full-ride scholarship recipients.

While these tactics cost schools somewhat in lost tuition, the schools make up for it with incoming transfers of upper-class students. The theory is that, if a school is known for weeding out one-third of its 1L students, it must produce quality lawyers. This increases demand for the school and prestige in the legal community, which in turn drives up tuition. This system, like the legal profession itself, is unforgiving and harsh, but surviving the process is a badge of honor. Also, as I mentioned previously, schools also don't refund tuition if you fail out.

Most law schools grade on a strict bell curve. Professors are limited by how many As, Bs, and Cs they can distribute. It's not just how well you perform; it's how you perform compared to the rest of your class. If you make the cut, you will be ranked against your classmates. That ranking will be at the top of your resume (if it is worth showing) and will follow you for the rest of your career. The top 10 percent of the first-year class will be invited to the school's prestigious Law Review.

I knew some students who returned for another try after they didn't make the cut. This was surprising, given the cost of tuition, but I respected their tenacity. However, some people simply do not have the work ethic, aptitude, intellectual capacity, or test-taking ability to make it in law school, and a few of those who repeated their 1L year failed a second time. If for any reason you don't make the cut, you should seriously reconsider whether it's worth another try, or if you might find more success and fulfillment elsewhere. Of course, trying again may be the right choice if you fail due to personal issues (like an illness, a death in the family, or some other emergency). But if you feel pressure from a parent, relative, significant other, or your own ego to keep trying at all costs, and your gut says otherwise, that in itself is worth examining.

Chapter 5

YOUR FIRST-YEAR COURSELOAD

ALL FIRST-YEAR COURSES will be assigned to you, and you will not select any electives until your second year. Despite any future specialization goals, every 1L must take the following courses: Contracts, Criminal Law, Torts, Real Property, Civil Procedure, and Legal Skills (the name of this last course varies by school). Each of these courses, except Criminal Law and Torts, lasts two semesters.

These core courses are absolutely critical and serve as the foundation for all future courses. For example, Real Property provides a foundation for courses such as Bankruptcy, Trusts & Estates, Land Use, and Environmental Law. Contracts provides a foundation for Corporations, Entertainment Law, Sales under the UCC (Uniform Commercial Code), and Negotiation. Criminal Law is the foundation for all criminal courses. Civil Procedure is the foundation for all civil courses.

Each school has unique graduation requirements, but you will generally be free to select your courses as a 2L and 3L depending on what area of law you plan to pursue. Unlike college, you will not pick a major, but you can tailor your electives and bar courses to favor any practice area you want. I didn't want to pigeonhole myself because I was interested in so many things, but I knew I wanted to do civil litigation, so I tailored my courses to be litigation-centric.

Not only does the first-year curriculum provide an important foundation for your legal knowledge, these courses are also heavily tested on the bar exam. If you thought you'd get a reprieve from bar exam stress during your first year, you were mistaken. You will officially begin studying for the bar exam in your first semester of school.

Now, let's look at each of the 1L courses in detail.

Contracts

The Contracts course covers the laws governing formalized and enforceable human relationships. As my professor Thomas Barton stated on day one of my first year, "A contract is a promise the law will enforce."

I'll be honest: Contracts was my least favorite class, and thus my lowest grade. Unlike Torts and Criminal Law, the subject matter in Contracts was mercilessly dry. There is just no way to make the Uniform Commercial Code engaging; no matter how hard I tried, I couldn't summon enough interest to properly learn how damages are calculated when a vendor fails to fulfill deliveries. Having said that, the principles of this course will be applicable in *every* area of the law (even criminal law), and are equally applicable to non-lawyers in the business world. Obviously, this subject is critical to students who want to enter corporate, entertainment, labor, and sports law. In fact, any transactional (non-litigation) law practice will primarily involve contracts. By extension, this course will instill some degree of business acumen.

I regret not trying harder in Contracts. My grade suffered

because the subject matter just didn't hold my interest. My overall first-semester grades were in the top tenth percentile of my class, but I got a lowly 74 in Contracts.

Knowing what I know now, I would have taken this course more seriously. Ironically, my worst grade in law school became a big part of my practice. I now deal with contracts every day as a business attorney, both in the litigation and transactional context. Contracts are the foundation of everything I do. Many lawsuits begin because a contract was breached, and most lawsuits end with a contract being created (called a "settlement agreement"). Almost every case I litigate involves some element of contract interpretation, performance, damages, and defenses. I constantly analyze contract issues, regardless of the nature of the lawsuit, and a large percentage of cases turn on whether a contract exists and what the contract does or does not say. Most of my initial consultations go right into contract analysis, as that is where I begin analyzing the merits of the case.

While studying Contracts was certainly dry, especially compared to the material I read in Torts and Criminal Law, the practice of business law is exciting and lucrative. So hang in there, and apply yourself even—especially—when Contracts is putting you to sleep.

Criminal Law

Unlike Contracts, Criminal Law was never dull. The course literally opened with blood and guts. My first reading assignment was about a man who beat his pregnant wife and caused a miscarriage, and the issue was whether he could be liable for the murder of the fetus.

Don't get me wrong: the fetus-murder case was disturbing

and not particularly fun to read, but I was excited because I knew this class was always going to be interesting. I never aspired to become a criminal lawyer, but this course held my interest, and that translated into a good grade.

Criminal Law teaches about the various crimes and their defenses. Each crime has certain elements which must be satisfied before the crime can be established. Each element is laden with definitions, exceptions, sub-elements, and public policies. You then turn to the "affirmative defenses" for the crimes—the situations where liability is eliminated or mitigated, even though all the elements of the crime were satisfied.

This course is pure memorization and issue-spotting. What are the crimes? What are the elements? What are the defenses? What are the applicable public policies served by these laws? If you can spot the issues and answer these questions in essay format, you'll do just fine in this course.

You'll also learn antiquated principles having little application to modern life. For example, common law burglary consists of four elements: (1) breaking and entering (2) of the *dwelling* of another (3) *at night* (4) with the intent to commit a *felony* therein. Of course, in modern society burglary can occur during the daytime, at a non-dwelling, and there does not have to be felonious intent. That is not the point. The point is to teach you to spot the issues, do the legal analysis, and think like a lawyer. You will also understand and argue the law better if you can trace its evolution over time, and your casebook will provide historical perspective.

As a 2L or 3L, you will take a course called Criminal Procedure (known as "Crim Pro"), which is tested heavily on the bar exam. The fact patterns mostly involve whether a piece of incriminating evidence is admissible in court, depending upon how the police obtained it. Crim Pro analysis requires an understanding of the underlying crimes and their defenses—which, as you now know, you will learn in Criminal Law. Bar exam essay fact patterns will require you to analyze both Criminal Law and Criminal Procedure together. It doesn't matter if you never intend to practice this area of the law; you will need to master this material to pass the bar.

Torts

This was another fun course with a lot of crossover from Criminal Law. A "tort" is a civil wrong, an act for which there is civil (as opposed to criminal) liability. This means the defendant pays money rather than going to prison. Some acts—such as battery, false imprisonment, or theft—can be both a crime and a tort.

Your Torts casebook will be filled with shocking examples of things that can go wrong in modern society. I took this course in the year 2000, and am sure the casebooks have been updated to include matters involving internet and social media disputes. Regardless, every conceivable calamity has already happened. I once read an insurance coverage case about a man who accidentally shot his passenger while driving: He modified the gun to create a hair trigger, then shot the gun out the passenger window while rabbit hunting. You can't make this stuff up.

Long story short: whatever stupid depravity or carelessness your mind can conjure has likely already happened—and you'll probably find it in this course.

If you want to be a litigator, you will need a firm understanding of Torts. Much of the semester will focus on the subject of Negligence. Negligence will take you to some interesting places, as humans have infinite capacity for stupidity and carelessness.

The legal analysis in Torts resembles Criminal Law, but Torts is heavier on public policy considerations, which can swing arguments either way. As a matter of public policy, is it desirable to hold certain people accountable for certain injuries? Who is liable when multiple people are involved in the cause-and-effect chain? What kind of monetary damages would deter careless or callous conduct in the future? This course makes you take a hard look at the society in which we live and how people are held liable for their actions.

As in Criminal Law, analysis in Torts often follows the elements. For example, Negligence occurs when the defendant owes a duty of care and the duty is breached, resulting in the proximate causation of damages. When you take Evidence as a 2L or 3L (another course heavily tested on the bar exam), the fact patterns often involve evidentiary issues associated with torts.

Real Property

This course begins in the Middle Ages in England, back when property was symbolically conveyed by delivering a handful of dirt or a twig from the land to the purchaser. Much of your time will be spent navigating English cases from the 1700s; unless you have a background in Regency-era English, you will have to re-read the cases again and again to grasp the Shakespearean judicial prose. These ancient cases are the backbone of our present real property laws. However, that doesn't mean that this course isn't useful.

Many concepts from the Middle Ages still apply today, including land ownership and conveyance of title, so you'll learn about the evolution of the law. This is a very dense course and will require the bulk of your study time. While there is some tort-like elemental analysis, such as adverse possession and easements, Real Property is filled with mystical and mysterious concepts that many lawyers do not understand.

Civil Procedure

Unaffectionately known as "Civ Pro," this class will make life very difficult for you.

I once played a round of golf during my second semester and got paired with a random guy. I mentioned something about my Civil Procedure class, and he responded with, "Yeah, it's important to be civil." I didn't bother correcting him, but this class has nothing to do with civility. This is where you learn about civil litigation—meaning, how to work a lawsuit.

The course begins in the ivory tower, learning about lofty concepts such as personal jurisdiction and due process. It then moves to the highly technical Federal Rules of Civil Procedure (FRCP). The FRCP applies in all federal courts across the United States, while each state has its own rules of civil procedure applicable in state courts. You will be expected to know the FRCP intimately. Most states model their codes on the FRCP, so understanding the FRCP can help you adapt to practicing in any state court. Sometimes, federal courts will apply federal procedural law and state substantive law (such as tort or contract), and there can be conflicts of law where multiple states' laws potentially apply. There will be multiple parties on each side, with counterclaims against each other and against third parties, and you will be asked to analyze jurisdiction, venue, and the mechanics of motions to dismiss and discovery.

Here, you will be introduced to case law authored by the U.S. Supreme Court; this jurisprudence dates to the country's founding. Supreme Court cases can span twenty-plus pages and are quite dense as the rulings get muddied with concurring and dissenting opinions. Supreme Court opinions are dense and verbose, so the opinions can drag on and on, making it difficult to spot the rationales.

Even if you know substantive law (such as Contracts or Real Property) cold, you're dead in the water if you don't know Civil Procedure. Procedural errors can derail an otherwise meritorious case and be a major malpractice trap for the unwary lawyer. Attorneys can be "out-lawyered" procedurally even when their cases are sound. I regularly practice in federal court, and this course is the foundation for how I make my living today.

Without understanding civil procedure, you cannot represent a client in any contract, tort, real property, or other civil action. Courses such as Torts and Real Property are theory-based and philosophical, but Civ Pro is more of a practical, vocational course. You will learn how a civil lawsuit is commenced, how the court obtains jurisdiction over the case and the parties, how the complaint is served, proper venue and parties, how a complaint is drafted, discovery, and motion practice; in other words, how a lawsuit works.

People are allowed to represent themselves in most lawsuits. You do not need a law license to represent yourself; you only need a license to represent *someone else*. Self-represented parties are known as "*pro se*." I have litigated and observed many *pro se* cases. It usually ends badly for the *pro se* party because they don't comprehend what is happening—they don't understand civil procedure. First-year Civ Pro is where you become separated from the *pro se* herd. You need to know civil procedure if you are to have any success in litigation at a civil law firm.

Even if you're a genius at torts issue-spotting and legal analysis, you aren't much use to a law firm if you don't understand Civil Procedure. Civil Procedure is how Torts, Real Property, and Contracts are *applied.* As you can see, these courses are interrelated.

Civ Pro is tested heavily on the bar exam, and it's one of the most important courses in the curriculum. You really need to apply yourself in this course.

Legal Skills

This course has different names at different schools, but they all cover the same material. This course is even more vocational than Civil Procedure. In Legal Skills, you will learn how to work as a law clerk and what lawyers actually do in practice. While other courses teach you the law and how to *think* like a lawyer, this course teaches you how to practice law, including research, writing, and oral advocacy. Regardless of your intended specialization, this course will be the first piece of preparation you'll receive for practicing law in the real world. It literally teaches you how to be useful to a law firm.

The research aspect begins with learning how to brief a case, a foundational skill for any law student. This is the process of identifying the parties, the procedural status, the legal issues, and the rulings, and reducing this information to a one-page document. Experienced lawyers can quickly scan a case and identify these components. This skill develops from repetition. Before you can read a case, you have to learn how to find it; that is the art of legal research. Legal dramas and lawyer commercials always show official case reporter books adorning the background, but these are obsolete to modern lawyers, who conduct most of their research on the internet. However, a good Legal Writing course will teach you how to research the old-fashioned way before you are allowed to touch a computer.

Once you are freed from the tangible case reporter books, you are introduced to legal database research. Online research will shave hours from your research time if done efficiently. There are two primary database companies competing for your attention (and your future business): LexisNexis and Westlaw. Other options are available, but LexisNexis and Westlaw make their databases available to law students for free in the hopes that they will become paying customers upon graduation—kind of like how tobacco companies used to target youth with candy cigarettes.

After you learn how to locate and brief a case, you will learn to write. First, you'll learn to write a legal memorandum, where you will objectively apply the law to a given set of facts. Despite the casual name, a memorandum is a technical and structural document an attorney uses to guide strategy on a case or project. The supervising attorney will pose a question to the clerk, who will then research, summarize, and analyze the findings. The scenario is that you are writing to advise a senior partner who will rely upon your analysis to advise the client about their options. You will be assigned a random state and will have to research your issue exhaustively. Then, you will write the memorandum according to a strict format. (This is where the IRAC method is beat into your head.)

The memorandum is objective, which is different from advocacy. Memoranda are freeing to write because your job is to be open and honest about your findings and analysis, where the law is applied to the facts, and the client and attorney are advised on strategy. This project will take weeks, and it might feel like your floaties just came off in the deep end of the pool. However, as a real law clerk and attorney, you will be expected to complete these tasks in a matter of days—or hours.

After learning the art of the memorandum, you will upgrade to writing a legal brief, where you are assigned one side of an issue and must try to persuade the reader. This is much more exciting than writing an objective memorandum. At the end of your first year, you will have to research and write a motion or an appellate brief, and you will likely be paired with another student. You will exchange briefs with adversary classmates and engage in oral argument before a panel consisting of professors, practicing lawyers, or even real judges. The process is terrifying for everybody, but you must learn to enjoy the game to succeed as a litigator. After your first year, you will know whether you want to be a litigator or if you are better suited as a transactional attorney—in part because of what the process of delivering your brief feels like to you.

Long story short: if you find yourself hating your Legal Writing course (and not just your professor, which is different and may very well happen), you should seriously consider whether this is the right profession for you. This course teaches what you will be doing every day as a lawyer; therefore, it stands to reason that if you don't enjoy it, you won't enjoy the practice of law very much, either.

Chapter 6

WORKING WITH YOUR PROFESSORS

LIKE THEM OR NOT, your professors will play a huge part in your educational experience.

In college and in law school, I found that my success in each course often correlated with my relationship with each professor. Your success or failure literally rests in their hands. And while one would like to believe that law professors, being experienced legal minds themselves, could remain objective and distant from interpersonal dynamics, that is rarely the case.

Therefore, it's in your best interest to learn how to work with your professors regardless of your feelings about them personally. After all, you can't expect to like, be liked, or feel unconditionally supported by all of your future colleagues or employers, so why would you expect that from your professors? However, with some foresight, preparation, and self-restraint, you can earn the respect of even the professors with whom you don't get along—and that is the point of this chapter.

Push Points

Law school professors provide strong motivation for you to be prepared and do the assigned reading. In part, this motivation takes the form of "push points"—meaning that your overall grade for the course can be "pushed" up or down by a percentage point based solely on your preparation or performance in class.

If you are unprepared when called upon, the professor might put a little red dot beside your name. As long as you did the reading and can intelligently discuss the case, you should be fine; professors expect you to be nervous and get tripped up by the questioning, so don't get worried if you stammer a bit. You won't receive a negative push point simply for poor *performance*, but you could get one for lack of *preparation*.

Here is an example. Constitutional Law ("Con Law") is a required course at all law schools for upperclassmen and is tested heavily on the bar exam. The casebook is about four inches thick and full of long-winded Supreme Court decisions. When I took Con Law in my second year, the book publisher decided we didn't have enough to read already, so a supplement to the casebook was released. One day, I didn't get the memo that additional reading was assigned in the supplement, although I did the required reading in the main casebook. Of course, I was called on that day. The professor asked about the holding in some case I had not read, and I had no choice but to confess that I was unprepared. I was caught with my pants down (figuratively, of course). You just can't fake it when you haven't read the case.

With a smirk, the professor reached for her red pen and made a little mark on a document. I'll never know for a fact whether my grade took a hit that day, but I did feel my final grade seemed a bit lower than it should have been. I likely received a negative push point for being unprepared. I missed a reading assignment in the supplemental casebook and had the misfortune of being called on that day. It was nobody's fault but mine.

It's always frustrating when a minor mistake, coupled with the bad luck of being called on, results in a lower grade. However, negative push points are good motivation for you to keep up with the reading and be prepared for every class.

Some professors might give positive push points based upon good preparation and performance, but I suspect this is very rare. Most law students are well-prepared, and everyone who gets into law school is intelligent, so you will really have to stand out to get a positive push point. You're *supposed* to do the reading, so don't expect special treatment for doing what is required of you. (I may have heard Chris Rock's voice in my head right here. Look it up if you don't get the reference.)

My first-year Criminal Law professor gave us a freebie right before the final. He gave a positive push point to students who submitted a top-ten list of ways to eliminate crime. You would be insane not to jump on a free push point like this. My list consisted of a bunch of filler and fluff for one through nine, but number ten offered the following gem: In order to eliminate crime, we should abolish all laws. Without laws, there can be no crime.

Office Hours

All professors are required to keep office hours. These are set hours every week when professors are available in their offices to meet with students informally. At the beginning of every semester, you should create a centralized document with all your professors' office hours and office locations. This is a valuable resource that should not be overlooked.

Office hours offer you an opportunity to converse with your professors outside the pressure cooker of class. If you are struggling with a concept, having trouble keeping up, want input on a practice exam, or even want career advice, you can discuss these issues in the safety of your professors' offices, away from the judgmental ears of your classmates.

Professor Ehrlich, my Real Property professor, would never directly answer a question in class. Instead, he responded to every question with, "I don't know, what do *you* think?" I became conditioned to asking myself that question whenever I felt the urge to raise my hand in class. Office hours were the exception; Professor Ehrlich happily answered questions in his office.

As the semester progresses, you should keep a list of legal concepts you're having difficulty grasping or nuances you want to explore further. Keeping track of your problem areas will make you more organized when visiting your professors. This has the double benefit of impressing your professors (making them more likely to remember you) and helping you get the most out of your time with them. If you come to office hours prepared with questions, you will stand out and demonstrate respect for your professors' time. Don't initiate idle chit-chat because there might be a line out the door, but follow the professor's lead if he or she feels chatty.

You can also use office hours to discuss practice exams. As detailed in the next section, many schools make your professors' past practice exams, with model answers, available for checkout in the library. This is a *huge* resource. Sadly, too many students either don't know practice exams exist or are too overworked to take advantage of them. However, if you use this helpful tool provided by your professors, you will establish yourself as someone who is going above and beyond and dedicated to success.

I visited Professor Ehrlich after taking several of his practice exams. I told him about my struggles applying certain concepts together in a fact pattern, and he lit up. The Professor shared that when students can correctly synthesize the concepts (merging and applying concepts from different parts of the course in one fact pattern), their grades are catapulted upward—or, as he artfully stated, "My points meter starts spinning." To have my professor tell me, and *only* me, the secret for acing his exams was invaluable. I now pass this secret on to you.

Finally, office hours are an opportunity to realize that your professors are real people. They say that you can tell a lot about a poker player by how they organize their chip stack. The same is true for how a professor maintains their office. Certain professors are intimidating and cold in class, but once you've seen their family photos, their book collections, their clutter, the diplomas on their wall, and the personal knickknacks in their office, you will have a new appreciation for them as human beings. This helps reduce the intimidation factor.

For example, Professor Stiglitz was tall, lean, bespectacled, gray-haired, balding, and more intimidating than any other professor at Cal Western. However, at the center edge of his desk stood a Dr. Evil action figure in his gray suit, arm akimbo, with its pinky finger in its mouth. Seeing that for the first time, I nearly laughed out loud because I realized Professor Stiglitz really did look like Dr. Evil! To his credit, Professor Stiglitz apparently wanted his students to see he had a real sense of humor, and that he was not above poking fun at himself. You've likely heard the suggestion that, when you are intimidated by public speaking, you should imagine your audience in their underwear and black socks. From that day on, whenever Professor Stiglitz grilled students in class, or even when he grilled me, I imagined that the class was being run by Dr. Evil, and I was able to relax a bit.

Professor Stiglitz took himself and the material seriously in class, so it was refreshing to see him exhibit self-deprecating humor in his office. In fact, much of the intimidation you see in class is theatrics and tradition, a rite of passage for lawyers.

I visited another professor as a 3L while taking his Corporations course. His desk was covered in random papers consisting of notes, correspondence, periodicals, books, and newspapers. Not only was the desk a horrifying sight, but piles of papers were also oozing from his bookshelves, threatening to spill out on the floor. I felt stressed out just being in his office. An extremely messy desk says a lot about a person; I began to worry whether this professor had the focus to fully read my final exam. I imagined my exam on his desk, on top of an uneven pile of newspapers, coffee ring stains, and sandwich crumbs. Disorganized, distracted people with short attention spans need to have their attention grabbed immediately. If that doesn't happen, their minds will wander—or, they might lose your exam in the chaos of their own clutter. I realized that I needed to make my point clearly and concisely at the outset to keep this professor's attention. I like to think this worked since I got a good grade in his course.

Given the benefits, you really have no excuse not to pay each of your professors a visit at least once a semester. However, do not abuse the privilege. Some professors are stalked like rock stars by their students, and the hallways outside their doors might be filled with bodies waiting in line. While there will be times when you have to simply stand around and wait, some professors allow students to make appointments and/

or enforce strict time limits for each visit. Using your time wisely is another great reason to arrive prepared with specific questions and a clear purpose.

Practice Essay Exams

While practice exams are not a *direct* way of working with your professors, I consider them part of that spectrum.

Most of the final exams in your 1L courses, other than Legal Skills, will have essay sections and multiple-choice. This is designed to prepare you for the bar exam.

Practice essay exams are critical to your success. They are equally important to attending class and preparing summaries and outlines. (See Chapter 7 for more on this.) You didn't take the LSAT without practicing, right? Well, you should apply the same level of diligence to your final exams in every course in law school. Yes, every single one.

Essay exams require you to spot a multitude of legal issues in rapid fire, and you will have to *synthesize* them together into a coherent whole while under an oppressive time limit. There will be a dense fact pattern that touches upon much of the subject matter you learned during the semester, followed by specific essay question prompts.

Here's what all of this has to do with your professors.

As mentioned above, your school's library should (hopefully) maintain a collection of all of your professors' past essay exams. Some professors even file model exam essays from actual students. This is a goldmine of information about both the exams themselves and also your professors' expectations and preferences, so you need to take advantage of this opportunity. I cannot overstate the importance of taking practice exams and simulating examination conditions.

Check out these exams from the library like you would any book, take simulated exams in exam-like conditions (I often took them in empty classrooms with a timer), and then discuss them with your professors during office hours. (Bonus: they will probably feel flattered, and will certainly recognize your commitment.) If you pay attention, you will gain massive insight into your professors' examination style—the simplicity or complication of their fact patterns, their tendency to revisit certain subjects, and how they hide issues like Easter eggs.

Assuming you've done the other work all semester, this is the most critical step in your preparation for finals. Mastering practice exams will propel you upwards by dozens of ranking points, thus multiplying your post-grad employment prospects.

There is no better way to study than to compare your essay with a model essay because it shows what the professor has in mind while grading exams. However, do not read the model essay until you have drafted your own under simulated exam settings. Simply reading the model essays without first attempting your own robs you of a chance to sharpen your exam-taking skills and to see where your weaknesses lie. Moreover, reading someone else's work before you produce your own can cloud your thinking and mask areas where you lack understanding and need to focus.

Note: Although I'm primarily focusing on past essay exams here, the essay is only about half your grade. Most final exams, as well as the bar exam, also have a multiple-choice section. It is doubtful that you'll find past multiple-choice questions from your professors because they get recycled over the years, but you can find ample multiple-choice practice questions in the various commercial guides available at student bookstores.

So, go ahead and invest the twenty dollars in a multiple-choice practice book for each course. This is not an area to be frugal.

HOW TO WORK WITH PRACTICE EXAMS

The best way to use practice exams is to treat them like real exams. Much of my time in my study group was spent taking practice exams in exam-like settings. We commandeered actual classrooms after hours, timed ourselves, and then exchanged exams with one another for critique.

At some point, you have to put down the outline and jump into the deep end. The more realistic the simulation, the better prepared you will feel when it comes time to take the real exams. When you do your practice tests, include both the essay and the multiple-choice components using whatever resources are available to you. All you'll need is your laptop, a timer, and a distraction-free space. Timing yourself is critical because it will teach you to manage both your time and the pressure that comes from being timed. Comparing notes with your study group is also an excellent barometer for gauging your performance and identifying problem areas.

I also recommend wearing earplugs or noise-canceling headphones whenever you are doing a practice exam. I found them to be a powerful tool for enhancing focus. During a test, you will be surrounded by distracting sounds—clacking keyboards, moving chairs, sneezing, coughing, rustling papers, etc. And, if someone breaks down sobbing, you definitely don't want to hear that! (A friend experienced this during his bar exam.) I used earplugs for all exams, practice and real. During the one exam for which I forgot to pack my earplugs, I found myself overly-sensitive to sounds in the room, which was a big downside.

When my first semester finals approached, I had at least a dozen practice essay exams under my belt. A classmate asked about my preparation for finals, and returned a blank stare when I told him about my test-taking regimen. He knew the practice exams were available in the library, but he never got around to looking at them. Given the stakes and cost of tuition, I was puzzled by his lack of preparation. Honestly, since you're competing on a very steep curve, you want people like this in your classes, but I still felt bad for him.

By the time finals were over, I recall thinking, "I could not have worked any harder than I just did." As athletes say, "I left it all on the field/court/track." Accruing so much exam-taking experience before exams even began gave me a huge confidence boost. Anxiety muddies and slows your thought process and interferes with memory. Practice exams help keep anxiety in check because you know what to expect when the real thing comes. I put as much time into test preparation as I did in studying the underlying material, and it paid off in spades.

Professors On the Warpath

You will sit for a photo for your school identification card during orientation. This photo will likely end up in a seating chart in a manila folder on your professor's podium. This allows every professor to know everyone's name and face, and where they sit.

On the first day of class, you may sit wherever you want, and the professor will note your seat location during roll call. Your photo will then be glued to that space, which will be your seat all semester, and possibly all year. This is a compelling reason to get to class early!

You are a photo in a folder. When the professor calls on you, they will look right at you and call your name. There is nowhere to hide.

Professor Stiglitz—otherwise known in my memory as Dr. Evil—was my most intimidating instructor at Cal Western. Despite his sense of humor, his reputation for breaking down students was legendary. My first class was Legal Skills, and the professor chuckled menacingly when he said, "You all have Stiglitz for Civ Pro."

On the first day of Civ Pro, Professor Stiglitz opened with a deadpan lecture about how certain students are not cut out to be lawyers, and his mission was to weed those students out. Stiglitz then called on his first victim and gave us a taste of an authentic Socratic grilling. Imagine hearing that speech, then being the first person called upon in a room of well over 100 peers. We all felt like weeds, hoping we wouldn't be yanked out of the ground.

It didn't matter how you responded to Professor Stiglitz's questions. Regardless of your preparation, you were in for a grilling when he called on you. If you answered correctly, he would scowl at you, then cross-examine you until you tripped. Wrong answers were excusable because they were expected, but he would really tighten the screws if you gave an equivocal answer or one which made you appear unprepared.

Professor Stiglitz made students very self-conscious of how they spoke, and he had no mercy for those who became tongue-tied. One poor soul began a response with the word "basically," and Professor Stiglitz interrupted and chastised him for using such a nonsense word. He was right. The word "basically" is a useless filler, devoid of any meaning. It's the intelligent person's version of "um." How do you intelligently respond to Socratic questioning after the professor makes you feel like a total moron? The message was delivered so harshly that I banished the word "basically" from my lexicon, and it still hasn't returned more than twenty years later.

One day, Professor Stiglitz warned my class that he was in a particularly nasty mood because of an answer he'd received that morning. He'd asked a student to identify the state where a litigant was domiciled, and the student responded with, "Chicago." This clueless response was doubtlessly caused by nerves and/or speaking too fast (or simply ignorance about the Midwest), but Professor Stiglitz couldn't let it go. He was *pissed off*, and subsequent classes had to deal with the emotional aftermath of that poor student's mundane slip-up. I'm sure everyone was praying Stiglitz didn't call on them that day. I know I was. I also remember that day every time I say "Vegas" when I mean "Nevada."

However, as it turned out, this aggression was all an act. Professor Stiglitz was a totally different person during office hours. Not only did he have that Dr. Evil action figure displayed front and center, he was calm and respectful, and warmly greeted me as "counsel" when I walked into his office, making me feel like a lawyer walking into the judge's chambers. After our first private meeting, I began to see his behavior in the classroom as that of a drill sergeant preparing his soldiers for war. Even the best marksman needs practice to be able to hit the target with someone screaming in his ear.

In summary: Do not let a professor's condescending tone or demeanor throw you off balance. You *will* need thick skin to survive law school and the practice of law. What you experience with your professors will, to some degree, mirror what you will experience with opposing counsel and judges. Most judges have some modicum of civility, and they won't berate you for a minor slip of the tongue—I have been guilty of plenty of tongue-tied moments in court, and I haven't yet been hauled away in handcuffs as a result—but having power over people can make some judges (and some professors) lose perspective and become belligerent, condescending, or just plain mean.

Therefore, if you expect *all* questioning to be unfriendly and refuse to take it personally, you can focus on the task at hand without hurt feelings getting in the way. I have conditioned myself to take nothing personally, and have learned to view icy comments from judges as guideposts about my advocacy. You can learn a lot from corrections if you don't allow your ego or feelings to get involved.

Chapter 7

YEAR ONE SURVIVAL TIPS, PART I

THIS IS THE CHAPTER where I share my "special sauce"—my practical secrets for becoming an effective and successful law student. I recommend you read this chapter carefully, then read it again. You're about to learn the system I learned during orientation and then applied and refined over the next three years.

Here is a condensed summary of the system I employed to be a successful law student:

- ***Step 1:*** Do the assigned reading and brief every case
- ***Step 2:*** Take detailed notes in class
- ***Step 3:*** Summarize your notes from every class
- ***Step 4:*** Consult secondary sources
- ***Step 5***: Prepare your own outlines for every course
- ***Step 6:*** Create and use flashcards and Post-it notes
- ***Step 7***: Take practice exams

In this chapter, we'll unpack each of these study steps in depth. Let's begin.

Step 1: Do the Assigned Reading and Brief Every Case

This one is obvious. Read the stuff you're supposed to read. Every time. For every class.

And …

KEEP YOUR DICTIONARY CLOSE

One of the best tips I received during orientation was to buy a legal dictionary and always have it ready. You never know when a dictionary might come in handy at a critical moment. Your casebooks will contain many unfamiliar words, including some in Latin, and you need to know what you are reading.

It is important that you get an up-to-date *law* dictionary; your old Oxford dictionary will not do. Law has a language all its own, and judges—especially judges of old—use outdated prose and terminology and take twenty-seven words to say what a modern jurist might say in eight. Present-day cases routinely contain phrases like, "The demurrer to the second amended complaint was sustained without leave to amend." You might understand some words from context, but legal parlance is very technical and specific, so you can't always trust your intuition and reading comprehension. Don't try to infer or assume the meaning of an unfamiliar word from context. Stop reading and look it up.

Professor Stiglitz used to work his way down a row when students struggled during Socratic questioning. When one student couldn't recite the relevant facts of a case, he would move on to the next chair in the row. If you were indecisive or foggy, he might ridicule you a bit, then dismiss you and move on to the next wide-eyed student in line. Stiglitz liked to work the rows in this fashion, so you often saw your turn coming. One day he called on my friend Frank, who was seated right next to me. This meant I was one "um" or stutter away from being called on, so I intently focused on the question as if he had called on me. Professor Stiglitz used a word I didn't understand, so I pulled out my dictionary and looked it up. I wasn't trying to attract attention to myself, only preparing for when the questioning inevitably moved to me, and I didn't want to look stupid. My stressed-out page-turning did not go unnoticed, and Professor Stiglitz announced, "Mr. Ladegaard is frantically looking through his dictionary to find the definition of [some word I can't recall and probably now use all the time in practice]."

My heart jumped into my throat because I thought he was making fun of me, but in fact he was paying me a backhanded compliment. He then went on to say that all students should always have a dictionary handy, and encouraged us to look up unfamiliar words. Professor Stiglitz used my nervous preparation as a teachable moment. This is also instructive that you should always be paying attention in class, even while another student is being questioned, because professor can turn to you at any moment with, "What do you think, Mr./Ms. [your name]?"

In law school you will regularly come across previously-unknown words (often in Latin). When (not if) you encounter a word you don't understand while reading a case, stop reading and consult your legal dictionary. This is critical to your understanding of the material because the nuance of legal definitions can change your entire understanding of a case. Your law dictionary should therefore be in your book bag by default. The added weight is worthwhile. If the dictionary is out of sight, you're less likely to use it and instead revert to drawing inferences through context. That would be a mistake.

(On a side note, law school will expand your vocabulary

significantly, so you should train yourself to avoid legalistic words when talking with your friends, or else they will skewer you for the elitist snob you have become.)

Your dictionary will continue to be a resource even after you graduate. Several years into my career, opposing counsel wrote in a brief that my client's conduct "obviated" the need for insurance coverage. I had never encountered the word "obviated," and assumed by its root "obvi" that it was some variation of "obvious." I couldn't be bothered to look the word up, even though the word was foreign to me. I wrote in my opposing brief that counsel was agreeing with us, that coverage was "obvious." Fortunately, common sense prevailed, and I looked up the word before giving the brief to my boss to proofread. Turns out, "obviate" actually means "to render unnecessary." Because I couldn't be bothered to open my dictionary, I completely misunderstood opposing counsel's argument, and was about to submit a backwards analysis to the court based on my misapprehension of a single word. It would have been humiliating for me, my law firm, and my client had I not looked the word up.

The lesson? Never be too arrogant or lazy to look up a word in the dictionary. Never assume you understand an unfamiliar word from context alone. Law school is the perfect time to create this habit.

PERFECT YOUR BRIEFS

No, I'm not talking about your underwear. This is how you read a case as a 1L.

A brief can take many forms, but an effective brief is one that notes the case name, the procedural status, a quick summary of the relevant facts, identification of the legal issues, and a discussion of the rulings and their rationale. Your Legal Skills course should teach you how to brief a case as one of your first assignments. You might even learn this skill in orientation.

When I began creating my own briefs, I also added a section for my own questions about the case and my notes on issues that confused me (which happened all the time and still does today). In my first year, I created a simple word processor template, saving each case brief as an individual file. I then printed each brief and filed it in my three-ring binder for each class. It felt like I was creating my own law library. (Yes, this was very nerdy, but at this point you should be beyond caring about such labels.) It also gave me a feeling of being organized and in control. When you begin working with briefs, you'll find your own systems for keeping things organized.

Briefing teaches you how to read cases efficiently, spot issues, and summarize the holdings. Many cases are lengthy, complex, and written in outdated prose, and cases often contradict each other. Briefs help you understand the law. Some professors even *require* students to prepare written briefs, and will call on random students to show their briefs.

Briefs can also serve as a handy tool in class. As the professor commences the questioning, your brief serves as a resource to help you easily recite the answers to many common questions. You will look and feel prepared, and this will boost your confidence.

Upperclassmen might make fun of the briefing process, as will people who don't have the time, patience, or work ethic to brief cases. However, briefing will help you learn, understand, and remember the material, better prepare you for class, and keep you organized. Plus, your course outlines will practically write themselves. If you brief enough cases your first year, you will become more efficient at reading cases and spotting issues; then, you can go easy on briefing or even outgrow it as a 2L or 3L.

A lesser alternative to writing your own briefs is "book briefing," where notes are written directly in the casebook. I've seen other students create systems where they have highlighters in several colors, with each color having a different meaning (such as facts, issues, holdings, etc.). I personally think the multi-color system is too cumbersome and a hassle because highlighters have such a short ink life. However, many students must work during their first year, while others have limited time because of personal obligations; in such cases, book briefing can help students save time, and it's certainly better than nothing. However, an argument can be made against making too much of a mess of your casebooks, as they have some after-market value and, if in good condition, be resold to student bookstores for decent sums. So, if you have real time constraints and don't care about reselling your books, highlight away! Otherwise, do your briefs in the way I've described above.

In summary, briefing is an absolute necessity for 1Ls. Commit to the process and pay your dues by briefing the cases. There is no excuse not to.

Step 2: Take Detailed Notes in Class

Having made it this far in your education, I will assume you know how to take notes in class. More, I'll assume that you have your own system that works for you, including your own form of shorthand and the kinds of content you do or do not write down.

When I was a 1L in 2000, about half the class used laptops in class. I imagine that percentage is much higher now, if not

100 percent, so I'll assume you're taking notes on a laptop or tablet with a keyboard.

Assuming that you are a thorough note-taker and a competent typist, I've got some general advice for you. You don't need to write down everything that is said in class. You aren't a court reporter, and your job in class is to be engaged, listening, and learning, not transcribing. Just as you must spot the issues while reading cases, you must identify and take notes on the salient material in class. (That said, if you're a great typist and transcribing actually helps you learn, do your thing.)

Some professors break from the Socratic method and share stories from their time in practice. These battle stories were among the more enjoyable and educational moments in class and lowered the temperature from the Socratic interrogation. When your professors share stories from their careers, stop typing and just listen. I still remember some of my 1L professors' stories today.

I do recommend that you take notes on the cases and concepts that are discussed in class, as they will likely show up on the exam. Also note any questions you've got about the material, as well as breakthroughs and epiphanies, which will happen all the time. If a concept stumps you, you should absolutely flag it so you can supplement your studies. (Use the highlighter feature, bold it, or use an asterisk, whatever works to get your attention.) I also suggest you notate your personal reflections, thoughts, and questions separately from your regular notes. You might precede such musings with an asterisk or type them in italics, whatever works for you. Just make sure they stand out so you can find them easily. This is also a great way to organize material to discuss with your professor during office hours. As I shared earlier, if you ask a straightforward question in class, a true Socratic professor might respond with,

"I don't know, what do *you* think?" Log your questions in your notes, then discuss them during office hours.

Once your notes are in digital format, however they get there, do your best to keep them organized. I had a master (root) folder for each course, with each containing three files: Class Notes, Summaries, and Outlines. I strongly advise you to keep your notes for each class in a single file. Each day, go to the bottom of the document, enter the date as a header, and take your notes for the day. Maintaining individual files for each day of each class is too cumbersome, as your computer will become cluttered with hundreds of small files over time. Plus, with your notes in a single file, you can easily search your material like a database, saving you time when creating outlines.

Step 3: Summarize Your Notes From Every Class

My Real Property instructor, Professor Ehrlich, required us to prepare written summaries of each day's material. He randomly called on us to read from our summaries and gave negative push points if we were unprepared. I saw the value of summaries early on, and dedicated myself to summarizing *every* class, not just Real Property where it was required. I figured Professor Ehrlich knew what he was talking about, so why limit that advantage to one class?

By summarizing each day's material, writing as if I were explaining the material to a layperson, I was better able to process and understand the material. It also forced me to face the material I did not understand. The summaries became a forum for documenting the issues where I needed help, thus preventing me from sweeping problems under the rug or forgetting about them until exam time. While I would notate my areas of confusion in my class notes, I dove a bit deeper in my summaries. Sometimes I would figure it out, and other times I would just get better at articulating why I was confused.

Each summary was just a couple of pages long. As with my notes, I created a single Word file for each course, titled "Summaries," then separated each class by date inside the document.

Don't overthink your summaries or put too much time into them. Think of the summary as a living diary for each course. This will create another step for you, yes, and you will fall behind at times, but this will pay dividends when you make your outlines and during finals.

I confess that I sometimes struggled to keep up with this self-assigned task, but never more than a week or so. However, my summaries made my job easier as finals approached because my outlines were much easier to write, and I used that extra time for flashcards and practice exams.

Step 4: Consult Secondary Sources

As described in Chapter 4, you should consult secondary sources like commercial outlines and (occasionally) hornbooks. The timing is up to you, but if a concept in the casebooks or discussed in class is confusing to you, a commercial outline might explain it in a different way and the subject matter might click for you. You might do this after your assigned daily reading, as a supplement, but you probably won't have the time to read secondary materials this often, as you'll spend most of your time as a 1L reading and briefing cases.

I recommend that you consult the secondary materials

when you're stuck on something and need another perspective. Commercial outlines are also useful while drafting your own outlines, but be careful to avoid just copying them; the whole point of an outline is the act of creation. You learn the most from making it, and relying too much on outlines made by others can deny you this educational opportunity.

In summary, use secondary materials as supplements, to deepen your understanding, and to help troubleshoot. They can help you piece everything together and can clear up confusion, but don't rely on them too heavily.

Step 5: Prepare Your Own Outlines for Every Course

The outline is a dense document where you clearly identify the rules, their policies, elements, exceptions, and defenses for each course. This a long-form outline, with headers and subheads, and you should do this for the entirety of every course. You should work on your outline throughout the semester, not just at the eleventh hour before finals. Whenever the course moves onto new subject matter you should, in theory, prepare an outline for the section just completed. Feel free to review your friends' outlines and commercial outlines, but do not let them become a substitute for preparing your own.

Outlines are different from summaries in that they are structured in headings and subheadings. While outlining the course material, you will need to synthesize disparate and related concepts. You literally have to figure out what goes where, and the learning occurs in the organization as much as the substance you write. I outlined almost every class in law school—but like most others, I was burnt out in my third year and my tank was empty. In my last semester, I borrowed a friend's outline for a Tax class I seldom attended, violating my rule about creating my own outlines. Let's just say my grade in that class did *not* help my GPA and class rank. The one class I did not outline was my lowest grade in all of law school. That says a lot.

I recommend you watch the 70s classic *The Paper Chase* before starting school. In this film, a Harvard Law study group bands together and delegates outlines, with each member outlining a different course, with the objective of sharing them before finals. Egos get in the way and the group disbands before finals without anyone sharing their outlines. This is a great model for how *not* to prepare for finals. Learning comes in the creation of the outline, not in passively reading one.

Step 6: Create and Use Flashcards and Post-it Notes

Professor Ehrlich once said that briefs, summaries, and outlines are the tools that you use to build a home. The home is your understanding of a given course, and the body of knowledge you'll eventually take to the bar exam. Each of these activities are tools, but you need to make these tools yourself. I went beyond Professor Ehrlich and created additional tools he didn't recommend, but they worked wonders for me. Those tools were flashcards and Post-it notes.

I don't recommend store-bought flashcards made by someone else. I'm of the opinion that homemade, artisan-crafted, organic flashcards, made by you, are always the most effective. Everything gets distilled down to this: class notes become summaries, summaries become outlines, and outlines become flashcards. Only after you've gone through these steps and compulsively used your flashcards during any downtime will you be ready for practice exams.

Some exams are "open book," meaning you can bring your outline. Other courses are "closed book," where you are expected to memorize everything. For closed book courses, it is critical that you reduce your outline to flashcards. This can be done on simple index cards. As I mentioned in Chapter 4, I hole-punched mine and connected them with a metal clasping ring. This kept them from flying all over the place.

You can prepare flashcards once your outline is completed, or do it as you go—but don't skip them. Flashcards help with memorization, which is essential for closed book exams where you have to spout off rules and elements without blinking. As with outlines, a lot of the learning is in the doing, so while you can buy flashcards (and sell them, too: I found a buyer for a batch of my homemade flashcards after my first year), you'll retain more if they are your own work product.

What kind of information should you put in a flashcard? Just read your outline and think of questions to ask yourself.

Here are some examples:

Side One	*Side Two*
What are the elements of [concept]?	List the elements
What are the exceptions to [concept]?	List the exceptions
What are the defenses to [concept]?"	List the defenses
What is the name of the case that held [concept]?	Name the case
What public policy is served by [concept]?	Describe the policy

I had law school down to a science by my third year. Class notes and briefs were condensed into summaries; summaries were condensed into outlines; and outlines were condensed into flashcards. By the time my summaries had been condensed into outlines and my outlines into homemade flashcards, I was ready for exams.

My flashcards were the most important aspect of my exam preparation. I reviewed them every which way—front to back, back to front, and at random. I even turned them into a game of *Jeopardy*, where I flipped the cards, showed myself the answer, and figured out the question.

My flashcards went everywhere with me. At the gym, I would flip through the cards between sets rather than staring into the mirror or watching television. This provided the added benefit of keeping me at the gym longer. I also gave them to my live-in girlfriend and asked her to drill me on them. She probably could have passed some of my courses after the time she spent doing flashcards with me. Working with her had many advantages. First, it prevented me from cheating and turning the card over. (You can't do that when the card is several feet away.) Second, it gave us something to do together, which we badly lacked because of my school commitments. Third, it helped her understand the volume of material I had to digest, so she never gave me grief when I studied. She would also ask questions about the material, and explaining the law to a layperson was a great way to evaluate my own level of understanding. (It was also good practice for my future career, as I now explain legal concepts to laypeople all the time.)

In summary, flashcards are an important tool in your kit. They're portable and versatile, and are an excellent study tool.

POST-IT NOTES

In addition to flashcards, I also employed another, weirder study method—for me, the best study method of all. As a visual learner with a photographic memory, I remember what I see, especially something I've seen many times.

From week one in school, I wallpapered my apartment with Post-it notes containing small nuggets of legal knowledge, usually the elements of crimes and torts. I placed the notes in locations where I was bound to gaze at them during mundane activities. This included the refrigerator and bathroom mirror, and all around the toilet. While brushing my teeth or using the restroom, I stared at the notes, closed my eyes to repeat the contents in my head, then stared at them again. This method of studying took no time out of my day, and as the semester progressed, I found that whenever I closed my eyes and thought of brushing my teeth, the elements of burglary would appear in my mind. Once the notes were memorized, I cycled them out with new notes on different subject matter.

You can do this from day one of school, and it's easy because it doesn't require any extra activity on your part. If you stare at something enough times, even unconsciously, it will sink into your subconscious. Whoever you cohabitate with might not like it so much (unless you live with another law student), and your quirky Post-it notes will give your friends ammunition to make fun of you, but it gives you an edge in the memorization of facts.

You have no excuse *not* to do this. Post-its take mere seconds to make, and using them takes no time out of your day, since you'll passively stare at them while doing domestic activities.

Step 7: Take Practice Exams

We covered this in depth in Chapter 6, so I won't repeat myself here, except to say this: take practice exams. Take as many as you can, from as many sources as you can. Use the tools I've already shared to make them more effective.

If your school's library has seven past exams for a given course, especially if they're from your professor, then take all seven exams. Just do one or two a day, as you need to take practice exams in simulated examination settings, and at least as a 1L, you won't take multiple examinations on the same day; they will be staggered out.

Think of your practice exams as training for the Winter Olympics. You wouldn't compete on a slope having only skied it once, would you? No, you'd do it over and over, as many times as you can. Test-taking is a critical skill, and this is what separates the top of the class from the rest—they are all excellent test-takers. Nobody is born with this skill, and it has to be practiced and developed. I want to say taking practice exams is the most important step to the system I'm teaching you, but practice exams will be a frustrating waste of time if you didn't do the work all semester and actually learn the material. However, learning the material cold, and doing all the reading, briefing, attending class, summarizing, outlining, etc., is not enough. You then have to apply that knowledge and develop your test-taking skills. Take this step seriously and simulate examination settings.

More Helpful Tips

Bear with me, because I'm about to sound *really* fussy.

In addition to my seven-step process above, there are

numerous other areas to which you will want to pay close attention. I've singled out a few of them below, starting with organization.

KEEP IT ORGANIZED

Even if you managed to skate through college with minimal organizational skills (like me), you will need to step it up in law school.

This might sound obvious, but organization is critical, especially in your first year. (It is also critical in your legal practice.) There is too much material in law school for you to be haphazard. This is the year when you will set up all the habits and systems that will carry you through your second and third years. You will also need to be able to access your information at a moment's notice, especially for open book exams.

You must keep your materials for each course separate. As noted previously, I kept a separate three-ring binder for each course, in which I stored all of my briefs, summaries, and outlines (each separated by a divider). I kept my homemade flashcards mounted on the wall with push pins. Each course was separated into sets of different cards. A good friend of mine who was working on his bachelor's degree copied my flashcard system, and his organized study area was impressive.

I am not quite as organized now as I was in law school, but I do have one of the cleaner desks of the lawyers I know. Disorganization is a major malpractice trap, and it looks bad to clients and coworkers. The habits I created in law school set me up to become a reasonably organized—and therefore well-prepared—lawyer.

LIVE BY YOUR PLANNER

As I attended law school in the early 2000s, I and most of my colleagues used old-fashioned, spiral-bound planners. Today I use Google Calendar to manage my deadlines and appointments, and I would probably use that application if I was a law student today. (I'm sure there are many other digital options for calendar management, but this is not my area of expertise.) I also currently use Asana for assigning and managing projects with my team in my legal practice. I am a big fan of the platform, and I imagine it would work just as well for assigning projects to yourself.

If you're using a mobile application to manage your calendar, it's probably already in your pocket or purse—but if you prefer a paper planner, be sure to keep it with you at all times. In addition to keeping track of your assignments, this is a good place to record your professors' office hours and office locations. In my planner, I recorded the daily reading assignments every day for every class. I also made a note for every class session that needed summarizing. When I completed any assigned reading or summary, I crossed it off. This system also came in handy for noting research and writing due dates in the Legal Skills course. Your final exam schedule will also go in your planner.

Given that I lived by my planner and accessed it several times a day, I started using it to record the due dates of my personal bills as well. Law school will consume so much of your mental and physical energy that it can be easy to overlook something like a utility or credit card bill. You improve your chances of staying on top of your personal life by including key elements like due dates, important social engagements, and your significant other's birthday in your school planner. This way, even with a ton on your plate, you will save yourself the pain and distractions of late fees, frozen utilities, or an irritated partner.

A note about digital organization: I attended law school before smartphones existed, and I'm sure there are all kinds of productivity, calendaring, and organizational apps out there. I didn't use them as a student, and this book is based on my experiences and lessons, so I am unqualified to teach about that. Even if I did summarize relevant applications, the book would quickly become dated and out of touch, so I'll defer to you to use any productivity applications that you deem useful.

HOW TO USE YOUR LAPTOP

At the outset of your 1L year, you will have to decide when and how to use your laptop in class.

In this day and age, bringing your laptop to class seems like a no-brainer—maybe even a requirement. Without a doubt, you will spend every class surrounded by people banging away on their keyboards. But in this area, as in so many others, you can choose whether to follow the crowd.

First, only attempt to use a laptop for note-taking if you can pay attention to the professor and type at the same time. If you are an effective and efficient note-taker, your class summaries will practically write themselves. Plus, typing the salient points requires you to follow the lecture much more closely; this helped me stay more engaged with the material. On the other hand, if you get distracted by typing while listening, generally have trouble focusing on more than one thing at a time, or are simply a poor typist, your laptop will be a detriment and not an asset. If you are an auditory processor, consider obtaining permission from your professor to record the class on real-time transcription software like Otter.ai, and extract your notes from those transcriptions when compiling your class summaries. That way, you can give your full attention to what's happening in the classroom without needing to look at a screen. I'm sure your professors, or the school itself, will communicate policies about the use of technology in class.

Second, make sure you back everything up to your cloud server(s) and external hard drive, every single day. If possible, set your files to automatically back up every time you save them. As I mentioned in Chapter 4, you don't want to take chances with your data.

Finally, if possible, purchase (or create a plan to access) a backup computer. There is never a convenient time for your computer to fail—and, speaking from experience, your computer is guaranteed to find a creative time to remind you of its short lifespan. The hard drive in my brand-new laptop failed in my second year. I had to send it back to the manufacturer for warranty repair, and had to take handwritten notes for a bit, which was painful.

To maximize its speed and efficiency, don't keep non-school files—like graphics files, video games, your photo collection, or your entire iTunes library—on your school computer. Finally, ensure your charging cord never leaves your computer bag—otherwise, you risk running out of battery power mid-class because you forgot to plug in your laptop the night before. Most law school desks and library workstations have outlets, so you should be able to charge your devices anywhere you go.

MORE NOTES ON DEVICES

Watch Out for Thieves

One thing many law students don't consider is how attractive their laptops, phones, and tablets are to thieves.

While spending hours in the library, you will inevitably visit the restroom or strike up a conversation with someone away from your desk … and away from your devices. You could return to your desk to find them stolen. This happened to an acquaintance of mine when he took a restroom break. You've got a major problem if you lose your files and they aren't backed up.

It seems obvious, but you should also be very careful about walking away from your computer, even for a few moments. Some workstations in the library might be outfitted with a mechanism to lock your computer to the desk, but you need to have your own lock. I employed a lazier alternative: I simply placed the computer in my laptop bag, shoved it under the desk, and tucked in the chair. I'm not recommending you do this, but hiding your computer is better than doing nothing. Today, when I work remotely at a coffee shop or restaurant, I'll put my laptop in the briefcase, sling it around my neck, and take it to the restroom with me.

If your laptop is stolen, you will lose less time (and minimize your stress) if your files are backed up in multiple places, both in the cloud and on a physical memory stick or external hard drive. That way, you can access them easily from your backup computer and get on with your classes with minimal interruption.

Don't Rely Too Much on Your Devices

You cannot allow your laptop to be a substitute for thinking on your feet. You will not have a computer to assist you in court, and you won't have one in deposition (you can actually bring them to both places, but they're only used to access files, not when you're examining a witness—not that it would do you any good).

People today tend to rely on their devices so much that they feel like a fish out of water when forced to look up from the screen. In Civil Procedure, Professor Stiglitz once targeted a student for questioning, and she responded that her computer had crashed. This student got a thorough tongue-lashing because you cannot hide behind your computer screen. You're not exempt from Socratic questioning if your battery dies, and you can't ask for a continuance in court on the grounds that your computer crashed. When the professor calls on you, never use your computer as an excuse if you flounder.

While computers can provide a big advantage during exams, there is a dark side—your computer going haywire at the worst possible moment. If that happens, you're back to the Bronze Age with paper and pencil … as if finals weren't stressful enough. You will have done all your exam prep on the computer, but you have to be mentally prepared for the possibility of your computer crashing at the worst possible time. I saw it happen to a poor soul who wasted valuable minutes fussing with her computer and arguing with the proctor (who was not getting paid and didn't really care). Having a computer glitch during finals is your worst nightmare, and not using a computer is the only way to guarantee this won't happen.

I once was unable to use my laptop during a final exam because the exam software glitched out and wasn't working. I had to stay calm and collected as I switched to a handwritten exam booklet. My handwriting is awful. I was frustrated and upset, but compartmentalized my emotions enough to get through the exam. My grade might have taken a hit, but that was better than having an emotional meltdown because of a technology failure.

Distractions: Video Games and Social Media

Honestly, I waffled between talking about games as a pro or a con.

When I was in school, my computer came with basic games like Solitaire, Freecell, and Minesweeper installed. (Phones weren't quite so smart back then, so my only games were on the laptop.) For me, these games were a great way to fill my downtime at school—and there was a surprising amount of downtime. If I had a few minutes to kill before class and no friends were around, or if I just needed a mental break from all the reading, these games helped me relax and reset.

On the other hand, I found myself flipping cards on Freecell and blowing up mines on Minesweeper whenever I got bored in class. I can only imagine what the people in the rows behind me thought about my work ethic. With games like this, I was able to play while paying attention, and would quickly switch to Word to type notes when important points were raised.

Since I was in school, both devices and games have gotten a lot more sophisticated—but they still serve the same purpose. Even brain-development apps and puzzle games are not helpful if you can't keep your ears open while you play them. It's a judgment call for you about whether games on your phone or computer are a help or a hindrance.

Also, playing games on your phone is a hard no. You can't take notes as effectively on the phone (unless you're using an audio recording app as mentioned above), so there's no reason to have it in your hand.

Social media did not exist when I was in law school, and I can only imagine how distracting that must be. If you are an avid social media user, someone who mindlessly opens an app and scrolls without thinking (I plead guilty on this one), here's a hack I use when I'm trying to stay on task or am under a deadline: log out of the applications. That way, when you're tempted to scroll, you'll be faced with a login screen. Treat that extra step as a reminder from your higher self that social media is off-limits during class. Instead, use social media as a reward between classes or in the evening. You're trying to build a life here; the memes and notifications will be waiting for you later.

Notifications

Nothing is more annoying than listening to someone's device go "ding, ding, ding" throughout class. To avoid getting distracted (and also save the sanity of your rowmates), turn off all notifications while in class. This means silencing your devices during class, and also selecting "do not disturb" on your computer. No email is so important that you need to check it mid-lecture. If the world is ending, someone will (gasp) call you on your phone—which, coincidently, should *also* be silenced while in class.

I'm sure your professors will communicate strict rules about devices on the first day of class—but if you do nothing else, silence your laptop in class and leave your phone in your bag.

Chapter 8

YEAR ONE SURVIVAL TIPS, PART II

IN CHAPTER 7, we focused on the more practical, tangible aspects of surviving your first year. Now, lets dive into the mental and emotional aspects, which are just as important as the rest. Your mindset, and how you feel from day to day, will have a huge impact on your performance. You must get your head right in order to execute on the steps I described in the prior chapters. This chapter will help you prepare for the road ahead.

Treat School Like a 9-to-5 Job

It can be difficult to gauge how much time you should spend studying, especially while first adjusting to the flow in the first month of the semester. In orientation, we were told to treat school like a 9-to-5 job. This doesn't mean that you should pack it in and go home at 5:00 p.m. no matter what. Also, your day will likely start long before 9:00 a.m. Rather, I'm suggesting that, at the minimum, you should clock *at least* eight hours of study every day, including time spent in class. Activities like commuting, meals, and scrolling online between classes don't count.

You will have better odds of keeping up with the courseload if you treat school like a full-time job. Attend your classes, then have the discipline to fill in the gaps in your day with productive activities like briefing, summarizing class notes, using secondary materials, outlining courses, flashcards, etc. If you do this, you'll be fine. A full-time workday still leaves you time to work out, have dinner, and unwind before doing it all again.

There will be some days that feel "lighter" than others, but avoid the temptation to get lazy. Midway through your first semester, if you find yourself thinking that school is not as demanding as you expected, you probably aren't studying effectively or paying attention to the right things, and you might be in for a rude awakening during finals. If you can get into the habit of working at least eight hours a day, and integrate the study program I shared in the previous chapter, you'll give yourself a good shot at keeping up with the material. This pattern will also set up good working habits for the bar exam and in your eventual law practice.

Avoid Working if Possible

Your job as a law student is to attend class and study. As I've shared, being a law student, especially a 1L, is a full-time job. It's an all-day affair. Attending classes, doing the reading, briefing the cases, and drafting course outlines will consume your day. Even your social time will be mostly focused on your shared school experience. During the weekdays, there will be no such thing as spare time.

Now is not the time to seek real-world experience by clerking at a firm. Getting good grades and ranking as a 1L will help you get that coveted clerkship as a 2L or 3L. Unless you worked at a firm before starting law school, firms aren't looking to hire 1Ls anyway.

Luckily, I had the means to avoid working. I lived off student loans and found inexpensive housing twenty minutes from campus. I was fresh out of college and had no children, no mortgage, and (aside from those rapidly accruing student loans) little debt. As a result, I had the luxury of studying as much as I wanted without having to worry about the "real world." However, I was mindful that other students in my class had families and day jobs. Many law schools have evening classes for such students, who are typically on four-year programs rather than the usual three years.

I strongly advise against working in your first year, even in the legal industry. Aside from preparing for the bar exam after graduation, you'll likely never hear that advice again in your life, so enjoy it while you can. If work is an absolute necessity, you still need to cultivate a full-time mentality toward your studies, and that will require sacrifice in other areas. If being a lawyer is your dream, this is just temporary hardship in pursuit of the life you want to build. If you can sustain a day job and/or a family and still manage to succeed as a law student, you have my respect—and you certainly have the capacity to handle the rigors of real-life practice.

Find Healthy Outlets for Stress

While it's generally a bad idea to work during your first year, you absolutely *must* find time to unplug.

Whenever I had downtime during evenings or weekends, I worried that some other student was getting the drop on me. Instead of watching *The Practice* (one of my favorite TV shows back then), I felt I should be learning how to practice. I struggled with unplugging from my studies and being present with others. I guilted myself whenever I wasn't studying. I still struggle with work-life balance in my practice.

While that inner voice can be a powerful source of motivation, you have to learn to silence it sometimes. No one can endure three years of schooling, plus the bar exam, without taking some downtime to rest and calm your nervous system. Compartmentalizing your life is an important skill. You must shut off that law student chip in your brain occasionally and remember how to be a human being—how to be *you*. I have seen students at the top of their class who are devoid of any personality whatsoever; that's what all work and no play will do!

I cannot tell you what to do with your spare time; only you know how to keep yourself happy and grounded. However, here's a hint: the things you love to do are probably a healthy outlet for stress. I was lucky enough to have Fridays off most semesters. I picked up a resident discount golf card and played golf at an inexpensive municipal course every Friday. While walking the course and striking up conversations with total strangers, school was the furthest thing from my mind. I also surfed, read non-law books, experimented in the kitchen, exercised, and indulged in the occasional video game. Yes, I was still busy, but it was a different kind of busy—a busy that kept me feeling fulfilled. The point is, you need to take time for yourself and your loved ones. If you burn yourself out, you'll be no good to anyone, and your studies will suffer. Also, you can't learn and retain legal concepts when you're really stressed out. So, stay connected to yourself and tend to your happiness. This is just as important as all the study techniques I've been teaching you.

Consider this practice for life as a lawyer, and ignore this warning at your peril.

Job interviews are 50 percent about your grades and ability, and 50 percent about culture fit and whether the interviewers like you. If it comes down to a valedictorian with the personality of a carrot and a pleasant person who is likable and can write ... well, guess who's getting the job? Additionally, once you're out in the real world, you will also need to manage your stress levels and build downtime into your schedule—at least, if you want to have any kind of life outside of work. And you do want to have a life outside of work. You're going to be present for meetings, lunches, and even trips with coworkers and clients, and you won't get far if you aren't a well-rounded and likable person. Imagine how far you'll go in the world if you're a magnetic person who also happens to be a brilliant lawyer.

Impostor Syndrome

"Imposter Syndrome" is the feeling that, no matter how skilled or experienced you are, you still don't belong, you aren't good enough, and that you are an imposter who will be exposed.

We all feel like this sometimes, and imposter syndrome can appear at all stages of your career. You are certain to experience imposter syndrome at some point during law school, and guaranteed to experience it many times throughout your legal career. This feeling can be triggered in many ways, such as seeing a classmate perform well during Socratic questioning, or hearing someone brag about their superior study habits. However, don't assume that these things make them better or more advanced than you. You don't know everyone's story, and we are all haunted by failures, regrets, and lessons from our past.

Everyone in your class is intelligent and a hard worker. Given that, do you think you will excel further by being the smartest person in the room, or would you rather be surrounded by people who are just as smart as or smarter than you? Of course, the latter choice is obviously better—and you will certainly be surrounded by smart people in law school. Just know that when you feel a little inadequate, a bit out of place, or you wonder if you belong in that class or at that school, take comfort in knowing that the rest of your classmates feel the same way. Just use those feelings as inspiration to keep working and to employ the system taught in this book.

You're a beginning law student. You've never done this before. Therefore, give yourself some grace, patience, and love. A great rule of thumb is to give yourself the understanding you would give to a close friend. If your friend flubbed a question in class, would you call them an idiot, or would you be kind? Also, remember that fear of the unknown always makes imposter syndrome worse. The more you establish a record of doing the assignments, keeping up with the material, performing well in class, and excelling at exams, your confidence will build and imposter syndrome will crop up less often, and you'll be better equipped to work through it.

After over twenty years in practice, I still get that awful feeling sometimes. It usually crops up when I encounter an issue or challenges I haven't dealt with before. However, I've come to appreciate that this profession is all about learning from our research and experiences, and I know that impostor syndrome is either an illusion or a signal that I have room for improvement.

Take a Break—And a Nap!

Science has proven it: most of us are more productive and mentally aware after a brief snooze. I tend to hit a wall in the early afternoon, particularly after a carb-heavy lunch. ("Food coma," anyone?)

There are two cures for the mid-day slump: caffeine and naps.

Downing a cup of coffee or an energy drink provides a quick burst of energy and supports mental alertness. The downsides of caffeine are that it can make you jittery and cause you to crash afterward; that it is a diuretic, thus increasing your bathroom visits; and that it is a chemical solution to a natural problem.

Sleeping, on the other hand, costs nothing, is free of side effects, and is 100 percent organic. Don't get me wrong: I consume caffeine. But when confronted with the rigors of law school, I found napping much more effective. In fact, naps supercharged my focus and productivity.

The library at my undergraduate university had a room with several old couches. Students took full advantage by making themselves at home and napping in the open. As a college freshman accustomed to the rigid structure of high school, it seemed absurd that people would nap in the open at school. I was more accustomed to dozing under the cover of my hoodie. Soon enough, though, I started settling into the couch room for reading assignments, and since reading made my eyes tired, before long I was freely and unselfconsciously napping away. Ten to fifteen minutes was all I needed to recharge my batteries; after that, I was ready for my afternoon class. I felt grounded and clear-headed, and it didn't come at the expense of caffeine jitters and a bursting bladder. I felt sharp and attentive, and this enabled me to better engage with and retain the information.

This habit followed me into law school, where it assumed greater importance in my daily routine. Law school reading assignments can take a lot out of you. Reading, especially the small type sizes in law school casebooks, can make you fade quickly. When this happens, you will have a harder time understanding difficult material, and your ability to critically think and retain will be compromised.

The libraries at both law schools I attended had plenty of quiet places where I could put my head down for fifteen-minute siestas. USD's library had quiet upper and lower floors, away from foot traffic and conversation, where I could snooze (and study) with less disruption. I would then arrive at my afternoon classes awake, alert, and in a good mood. The only downside was that I slept through class a couple times. You can solve this problem by setting a vibrating alarm on your phone, and I've found that having an alarm set helps me relax and drift off.

If you can find a quiet place on campus, I highly recommend getting a few minutes of shut-eye when you feel the need. It will pay dividends in your ability to study longer and more effectively, as well as help stabilize your mood.

Disappointingly, my siesta habit did not translate very well into the practice of law, at least when I worked in law firms. I've had many coworkers storm into my office unannounced while I was checking my eyelids for leaks, and it was awkward, stressful, and annoying. Kicking my feet up in my office chair with a stack of paper in my lap, with my back to the door, never fooled anyone. I used to work with an obnoxious attorney who thought it was funny to sneak up behind me and clap his hands. (Not that his productivity was anything to brag about. He spent most of his day on Facebook.)

Napping in office environments was difficult and frustrating because I felt like I had to hide it. This kind of self-care practice isn't exactly encouraged or celebrated in the legal profession, and this is a shame. A twenty-minute afternoon power nap could make a big difference in production and profitability for everyone.

I'm self-employed now, and I'll take a short nap whenever the hell I want. You might not want to be around me otherwise.

If you're not able to take naps for any reason, the next best strategy is to take regular movement breaks. If you're regularly consuming fluids (which you should be), you'll be forced to take restroom breaks, and that's a great time to walk around and stretch your legs. Take the scenic route. Climb a flight of stairs. Give yourself five or ten minutes to move and stretch, and then come back to your desk.

Marathon study sessions are not an efficient or effective way to study. If you look up from a casebook and can barely see ten feet away, or if you have to re-read the same paragraph over and over, it's time to take a break. Take a quick walk, chat with some friends, get a drink or a snack, play a game on your laptop or phone—anything that hits the "reset" button in your brain. This can help refocus you and distract you from feeling tired. Getting good rest and avoiding alcohol the night before will also set up your mornings for success.

Join a Study Group

Much of my success in my first semester is owed to my study group. I joined a group of five guys. God bless them. I don't know if I could have handled the rigors of final exams without them. We gathered in study rooms and at each other's apartments on weekends and evenings, compared outlines, drilled each other with flashcards, took practice exams, and debated our way through difficult legal concepts. We kept each other on track and focused, but we blew off a lot of steam together and formed a special bond. We put ourselves through boot camp, and all but one of us became 2Ls.

As I've mentioned, an interesting aspect of being a 1L is that your classes are preselected, and you will see the same faces in each class. Midway through the first semester, you will pretty much know who your friends are and who seems to be putting in the work. That's a good point at which to find a group of reliable people you like and who seem capable of pulling their own weight to form a study group. Start out by meeting a couple of hours a week and put in more time as you get closer to finals.

Even the best study group is no substitute for doing your own work and preparing your own outlines. (Refer to my favorite law school move, *The Paper Chase*, to find out what happens when you rely too much on your study group!) Also, while you need to get along and vibe with the group, if you are clueless about the subject matter and not pulling your weight, you won't be welcome for very long. You need to be engaged in the material and be an asset for your group—and that means doing your own work, consistently.

That said, the most important thing is to find people whose company you enjoy. You are going to spend hours together in cramped quarters, and you have to be able to tolerate each other during incredibly stressful times. In retrospect, some people in my study group did not pull their weight, and benefited from me more than I benefited from them. However, I enjoyed their company enough that I attended all the group sessions, and this inspired me to study more than I would have on my own. Making myself accountable to others helped me be accountable to myself. That group was as important to my success as a 1L as my solo studies.

By the time exams were over, I felt like I'd been to war with those guys. We had bonded over an incredibly intense experience. However, our group dissolved after that first year.

One guy did not make the cut and had to take the semester off. Another found a girlfriend and we pretty much never saw him again. I tried to reform the group in our second year with one original member and some new people, but we couldn't recreate the magic. The vibe and connection just wasn't there, and we spent our study time goofing off and chatting. As a result, my grades and rank dipped in the second semester. I fell from the top tenth percentile to the top quarter, largely because the loss of my study group made me less disciplined. Top quarter is still better than three-quarters of the class, but it's a big fall from top ten.

The value of a study group can be further expressed by analogy. When I first started writing this book, I was working in a law office with six other lawyers. When I was grappling with a legal issue and wanted to strategize on a case, I would often seek out the other lawyers in my firm. You become a better thinker and a better lawyer if you can debate the issues out loud, with frank and open discussion, with people who can respectfully disagree with you and are not afraid to challenge you, or they might have experience or knowledge that I could learn from. In those days, the legal strategies in my cases were often the result of thoughtful discussion and debate with my coworkers, and it showed in our work product. Two or three heads together are better than one.

Working with a study group provides the same benefit. The difference is, instead of strategizing on a case, a study group works to understand the law and learn how to pass exams. Each of you will bring different perspectives and questions, and you will make each other better students. You will all benefit from your collective brilliance.

Choose wisely. Test drive some people, and don't give up until you find your crew.

If You Fall Behind

Have you ever had a class where every assignment you completed was from the previous week? Have you ever hidden your face in class because you didn't do the reading and didn't want to be called on? This was me in just about every class in high school, and more than a few times in college. But while those incidents were both embarrassing and frustrating, they didn't have a huge impact on my grades.

Well, as I shared earlier in this book, you will not be able to fake your way through this time around. Once you fall behind, you will have to work double time to catch up with the material. The law school train will not stop or slow down for you, and your excuses won't matter.

Falling behind can take many forms. Missed reading assignments, classes, or research assignments are relatively easy to deal with: just put in some overtime and catch up. If you have a great study group, this should not be a problem. Just ensure whomever you're getting notes from is a competent note-taker and understands the material. (And be sure to reciprocate when you can!)

The bigger issue with falling behind is a lack of thorough understanding. You will struggle if the course advances to new material before you have a good grasp of the current concepts. This can happen even if you never miss a class, complete all your summaries, and do all the required reading. Some concepts in law are simply harder to grasp than others. This is problematic because the concepts build upon each other. In Criminal Law, the entire course is built around the crimes and their elements, so you will struggle with material deeper in the course if you do not understand the crimes themselves. In Real Property, much of the course builds upon conveyances of title and the "bundle of rights" associated with ownership. Flawed understanding of these concepts will cause you to struggle with everything else that comes after.

Take it as a given that you are, at some point in your 1L year, going to feel like you are falling behind. No matter how smart you are, you will struggle, to varying degrees, with the majority of the information you encounter. If you find that you're having trouble understanding a concept, or how separate concepts relate, discuss it with your study group, read commercial outlines, or discuss the issue with your professor during office hours when the intensity and competition is absent. However, don't focus on past material to the detriment of remaining current.

Another option when you fall behind, especially if you are also struggling with the material, is to enroll in tutoring (if that service is offered by your school).

The pace of law school is meant to prepare you for real life. Falling behind in practice means missed deadlines, being unprepared at hearings and depositions, and even getting sued for malpractice. This can be fatal to your clients' cases and your career. If you can keep up with the material in school, you have a good chance of keeping up in practice—but if you're consistently falling behind despite your attempts to remain on top of the workload, consider that a red flag.

Despite my attempts to scare you, don't panic. When you feel like you're in over your head, just recognize where you are and make a plan for catching up. With discipline, hard work, organization, and focus, you'll be back on your feet in no time.

Chapter 9

EXAMS

MUCH OF YOUR GRADE for each class, if not your entire grade, is dependent upon your performance on the final exam. Each of the steps covered in past chapters build up to this moment. Final exams are the most pivotal moment of the semester, and we're going to set you up for success.

On the one hand, your entire semester has been building toward this moment, and your entire grade, plus the tuition you've paid, hangs in the balance. On the other hand, you'll need to put all of this out of your head and focus.

Examination rooms are intense environments. In fact, throughout the semester you will feel tension growing around campus as final exams get closer. That said, life and its problems do not stop because you're studying for finals or in the middle of exams. Anything that could go wrong might go wrong. You might experience or witness computer failures, traffic, illness, emotional breakdowns, arguments or spats between students and proctors, phones ringing, broken HVAC, parking lot repairs, etc. I once burned three-quarters of an entire test period writing two essay answers and totally missed a third fact pattern and essay. I got rushed and sloppy, and dove into analysis before looking over the entire packet.

Then, there are the things that go wrong on a macro or collective level. 9/11 happened when I was a 2L at USD. The semester had just begun, but the horror of that day hung over all of us like a cloud of smoke for months. On the one hand, it made passing the bar feel more urgent. On the other hand, it was hard to concentrate with so much fear and uncertainty in the air.

However, no matter what transpires for you, your peers, or the world, exams will go on, and you will need to be ready for them.

Exams usually take three to four hours, and the pressure will be intense. As you know from the Practice Exams section, exams can take one of, or a combination of, three forms: essay, multiple-choice, or practical. This is designed to mirror the bar exam.

Most exams involve both essay and multiple-choice, and these parts of the exam are separately timed. Some courses will have a practical where you are given a fact pattern that might occur in practice and are tasked with writing a memorandum or motion. This is "practical" because you're doing the act of lawyering.

Your class will be split between typists and longhand writers (as noted earlier, some people do choose to take their exams that way), and those groups will be tested in separate rooms. Whatever approach you choose, make sure you apply it in your practice exams as well.

The discussion below is critical information based on my experiences taking three years of law finals, followed by the bar exam. Final exams in law school are nothing like your finals in college or high school. It is a totally different game.

Open Book or Closed Book?

Whether or not an exam is open book or closed book will greatly influence the way you study throughout the semester. Open book exams require detailed outlines, while closed book exams require thorough memorization.

As an aside, my opinion is that open book exams prepare you for the practice of law, whereas closed book exams prepare you for the bar exam. As a result, I have mixed feelings regarding the degree of memorization required in law school. Some professors expect you to commit that three-inch casebook to memory. On the one hand, after working so hard to remember the material, you are more likely to spot issues on the bar exam and later in practice. My hard work in law school helps me in my present-day practice because (I like to think) I'm pretty good at spotting issues. Issue-spotting is a critical skill you will learn in school, and will be mandatory in any practice area. On the other hand, practicing lawyers generally don't need to memorize much—although I once had a bench trial where the judge admonished the attorneys for looking at notes during closing arguments, so memorization would have been handy there. In most cases, however, we can take notes into court and depositions, and we don't draft motions based on memory. I know legal concepts, but rarely commit case names to memory once a motion is done.

But, I digress.

Some professors will allow you to use your self-produced outlines during the exam for reference. Open book exams tend to be highly comprehensive; therefore, your outlines for these courses should have as much detail as possible. You should be intimately familiar with the outline, so you know what material is located where. This format eases the burden of memorization, so you won't need to spend time with flashcards (although I do still encourage the Post-it notes). For open book exams, you will want to include every legal concept and every case from the course in your outline, as most of this material will be represented in the exam. Some courses, such as Civil Procedure, also allow you to bring the Federal Rules of Civil Procedure booklet for reference.

Unfortunately, professors don't always publicize whether the exam will be open book. Some will give you a couple weeks' notice, while others might put the word out at the beginning of the semester. I've also seen professors feign indecision until late in the semester. This is one reason why it's a good idea to have solid outlines for *all* of your courses. Plus, as we've discussed, creating the outline over the course of the semester is how you really synthesize and understand the material. You don't want to be scrambling to prepare outlines while simultaneously studying for finals! The time before finals is for taking practice exams, using flashcards, and *reading* your outline, not *writing* your outline.

On the other hand, some professors expect you to memorize all the material. For such courses, your outline will be one tool out of many. Your outline will then get condensed down to flashcards and Post-it notes (see my tips in Chapter 7). Detailed and comprehensive memorization is the key to surviving closed book exams.

Regardless of whether the exam is open or closed book, your job is to spot issues, recite the rule, analyze, and conclude. (IRAC.) If you can't do that, it doesn't matter how great your outline is or how much material you have memorized. The attorney's job is to analyze, not just memorize. However, knowing whether the exam is open book or closed book will influence the way you study so you can use your time more efficiently—so be on the lookout for any announcements about how the exams will be conducted, and alter your preparation strategy accordingly.

Multiple-Choice

Between high school testing, the SAT, university, the LSAT, and practice exams, multiple-choice exams have become an inescapable part of your career as a student. You've had a lot of experience here already, and the same basic strategy of using deductive reasoning to eliminate wrong answers applies here as much as it did in high school. This section focuses on what to expect from law school multiple-choice exams.

In law school, each question on a multiple-choice exam will be in the form of a small fact pattern of one or two paragraphs. Each question is presented with four possible choices, (a) through (d), and your responses go into the same Scantron forms you used in high school. Sometimes you will see longer fact patterns with multiple questions.

Multiple-choice questions are tricky, confusing, and mentally exhausting. You might know the law cold, but your mind can only endure so many double negatives in a short time span. Professors will sadistically trip you up with word games that require more reading comprehension and concentration than legal analysis. Multiple-choice questions are also frustrating because we are taught as law students that black-and-white answers are rare, yet multiple-choice exams are exactly that. For each question, there is one right answer and three wrong ones.

This type of testing is mentally exhausting, and you

should pause at intervals to close your eyes, take a couple deep breaths, and reset before reading the next fact pattern. If you keep yourself calm, grounded, and centered, your focus and endurance will improve, leading to improved performance. The moments you lose while taking a quick mental break will be made up in improved productivity and efficiency, I promise.

For each exam question, slowly and carefully read the fact pattern, the question, and the potential answers. Each word has been chosen for a reason. For each fact pattern you read, pause and ask yourself, "What is the call of the question? What am I actually being asked to analyze?" You might be eager to start analyzing a fact pattern a certain way, but the question might skew your analysis in a different direction. You will get mind-bending questions like, "Which of the following choices is not correct?" While that might not sound too bad, it is *very* difficult when you are forty questions and thirty-five minutes deep into the exam. The multiple-choice answers also get gummed up with double negatives, and this sadistic word game slows you down.

As you know from being a student for many years, the process of elimination approach works best on a multiple-choice test. Cross out the answers that are clearly wrong and focus on the answers that are plausibly correct. Do your best to narrow the field to two choices, which at least gives you a fifty-fifty chance. Even if you see the correct answer right away, take a moment to read and cross out the wrong ones, just to make sure you read the question correctly.

Feel free to write all over the exam booklet. Make notes, cross out wrong answers, underline important facts, or doodle all over it. You will have to turn in the exam booklet at the end with your name on it, but only your Scantron sheet counts.

Essays

The other half of most of your exams will be in essay form. You will be given a lengthy and convoluted fact pattern, a mini-universe of information, and a series of questions. Every fact is inserted for a reason, and the professor expects you to spot the issues, identify the applicable law, analyze, and conclude.

The fact patterns are borderline humorous and they all start to sound the same once you've read enough of them.

Here's a common example of a Torts essay exam:

> *Connie Careless was driving down a quiet residential street, ten miles above the posted speed limit, and was operating her car stereo while head banging to heavy metal music. Peter and Paula Plaintiffs were on the sidewalks, having a heated argument about which Back to the Future movie was the best. Paula became offended and shoved Peter, but she was unaware that Peter had an equilibrium imbalance, which caused him to fall backwards upon the slightest bump. Peter fell into the street and was run over by Connie, who was looking at her stereo, although Peter was partially obscured from her view by a parked SUV. Paula was so shocked and upset by the vision that she ran into her home in a panic, but she fell when a stair outside the front door caved in. The staircase was manufactured by Claire's Stairs. The broken stair has a tiny warning sticker reading: "Caution. Do not use stairs in an excited or aggressive manner." Immediately after the incident, Claire's Stairs*

> *reinforced its stair design to be more resilient and enlarged the caution sticker.*
>
> *Question: Analyze the duties and liabilities of each of the parties.*

These kinds of questions are a free-for-all to break down everyone's potential claims and defenses. There's a lot of issues to spot and points to mine in fact patterns like that. These questions are rather fun to answer, and the wild fact patterns and humorous names bring a little levity into a stressful situation.

Criminal Law exams resemble Torts exams, but the actors are on crime sprees instead of gross negligence. Below is an example of a Real Property exam:

> *Zachary owned a property named Blackacre, where he lived next door to Penelope, who owned a property called Whiteacre, for twelve years. They were terrible neighbors. Zachary disliked Penelope's habit of playing drums late at night, so he constructed a bright yellow picket fence between their properties. Zachary was unfamiliar with the exact location of the property line, and he accidentally placed the fence two feet onto Penelope's property. Penelope actually liked the fence, as it complemented her flower garden, so she never objected to the fence. Zachary decided to sell his home six years later, and gave a grant deed to Juliette, who placed the deed in the trunk of her car. The next day Zachary got a better offer from Russell, so he gave a quitclaim deed to Russell, who promptly recorded the deed at the county recorder's office.*

> *Question: Analyze the rights and liabilities of each of the parties as it relates to their property interests.*

Contracts exams involve broken and half-performed promises; one promise is oral, another is written; one person is a minor and another has dementia; goods aren't delivered; one seeks payment and the other seeks performance. Contracts exams tend to be dry and are not nearly as fun as Torts and Criminal Law exams.

Civil Procedure exams are the worst, involving six parties in different states, everyone suing everyone, with nightmarish fact patterns involving personal jurisdiction, service of process, improper joinder, indispensable parties, compulsory cross-complaints, and subject matter jurisdiction. You will be expected to know the Federal Rules of Civil Procedure cold, and the exam will be highly technical.

You will be tempted to start writing immediately after reading the fact pattern, particularly in light of the time constraints. However, it is imperative that, before you start writing anything, you first sketch a quick outline of your analysis. This needs to be repeated: *do not dive into your answer without making an outline!* Write down the issues and make shorthand notes of the points you intend to make. It is through the outlining process that you will spot and develop the issues. With a rough outline done, the legal analysis practically writes itself. Plus, your writing will flow better, be better organized, and be more persuasive. Skip this step at your peril. The ninety seconds it takes you to sketch an outline will be made up for many times over in improved efficiency.

Outlines are even more critical if you choose to handwrite your exams. Unlike the typists, you won't have the option of deleting, cutting and pasting, or inserting a new sentence into a prior paragraph. Therefore, you will need to know how you plan to articulate your response *before* you start writing. You need to be clear about what you want to say *before* you start writing.

Your professors will have a checklist of issues they expect you to hit in your essays. A couple of my professors actually showed them to me. You will get some points for simply identifying the issues and correctly citing the applicable law. Most of the points are in the analysis, and the professors want to see you synthesizing a wide array of concepts, meaning you spot issues from disparate concepts from the semester and discuss the interplay. You'll also get points for concluding regardless of your conclusion, so do not miss out on those easy points. Spotting the issues is, of course, the most important skill, as you can't cite the law, analyze, and get those attendant points if you've missed the issue altogether. The skill of issue-spotting comes with experience and repetition—experience from watching your classmates get grilled using the Socratic method in class, and repetition from reading and analyzing hundreds of cases.

My first-semester Legal Skills primarily taught legal analysis, and it used the random topic of common law marriage as an example for how legal analysis is conducted. We literally studied common law marriage for weeks, with research and writing assignments. We were then tested on it, just like a regular exam. The topic was irrelevant, but it served as a focal point for how to perform legal analysis. The mid-term exam for that class had a common law marriage fact pattern about a couple, and we were asked to analyze whether they were married. Buried in the fact pattern were facts about the man's other relationship, and there was a hidden second common law marriage fact pattern. This second fact pattern counted for half the points in the exam, so merely spotting that issue catapulted me above half the class. I know this because the professor later told me that most of the class didn't pick up on the second marriage issue, which obviously nullified the primary one in the text.

If you're a great issue-spotter, essay exams will reward you; if you're a bad-issue spotter, essay exams will punish you. Luckily, sticking to the basic IRAC formula will help you navigate even the most convoluted fact patterns and stay on topic. Even if you don't understand the fact pattern or the question, or if you struggle with a certain area of the law, *follow this formula* and you will survive essay exams.

Another basic tenet is to *answer the question!* You will undoubtedly spot issues while reading the fact pattern, and it can be tempting to immediately start writing about the issues you see. However, points are not awarded for discussions that do not answer the question presented. Questions that ask you to analyze the duties and rights of everyone are a free-for-all, and everything is fair game. However, questions that focus on a certain issue or party will require you to be more specific, so do not waste time writing about issues that are off-topic. If you are asked about the duties of Connie Careless, don't veer off on Paula Plaintiff. Not only will you get zero credit (no matter how brilliant your analysis), you will consume precious time that could be used on other essays.

Practical Exams

While every final exam will contain multiple-choice and essay components, you will encounter practical exams in some, but not all, of your courses. However, they are absolutely tested on the bar exam. When I was in school, about 25 to 33 percent of my exams contained a practical component.

Practical exams give you a fact pattern and a confined universe of facts and materials to work with, like a contract, client documents, or fictitious legal authorities. You will then be asked to perform some act of lawyering, like writing a memo, motion, or correspondence.

I think it's great that schools and bar examiners test for the creation of actual legal work, because this is what you will be doing upon graduation. You can't really prepare or study for a practical exam; you just have to apply the skills you learned throughout the semester, like spotting issues, analyzing in IRAC format, and creating some tangible work product. If you know the material, have learned how to "think like a lawyer," and can perform written analysis of materials given to you under a tight timeline, you should be fine. This is, after all, what we do as lawyers

Time Management

Here's my advice regarding time management: use all of the allotted time, while always being aware of how much remains.

For the multiple-choice section, try to complete roughly one question per minute. A good strategy is to begin by answering the questions you feel confident about and defer the rest. If you are stumped by a question for more than one minute, make a note in your exam booklet (remember, you are free to write all over it) and return to the question later. Once you've answered all the questions where you have certainty, go back to your deferred questions and see which ones you can narrow down to two possible answers. Then, hit the tough ones that you've only narrowed down to three choices. If you have no clue at all, a good approach is just to run with the first answer that appeals to you. Anyone skilled in test-taking can affirm that your gut instinct about the correct answer is usually the correct one.

For the essay portion, skim the exam booklet and divide your remaining time by the number of questions, then stick to it. If you've got an hour to answer four essay questions, allocate fifteen minutes per question—and don't forget to outline! If you hit the time limit for a given question, have the discipline to wrap it up and move on to the next question. Even the most brilliant and polished answer to a question, worthy of publication in a law review article, will not offset unanswered questions elsewhere in the exam. You are better off partially answering all questions, while touching on as many issues as possible, rather than misallocating your time and answering only a few. You can always return to a prior question if you have time remaining after finishing the rest.

I managed to follow these rules until my last semester of school. During a Tax exam, I neglected to skim the exam and allocate my time between the essay questions. I also neglected to outline or read ahead, as was my usual practice. As a result, I spent an inordinate amount of time on one question, lollygagging, dilly-dallying, and pontificating about tax deductions. I really nailed that question and was proud of myself. With five minutes left, I was feeling great—until I turned the page to find a new fact pattern and question I had missed entirely. Trying not to panic, I did my best to focus and hit enough issues to score some points, but the damage was done. I spent the final seconds writing the following self-deprecating note to the professor: "As you can tell, I clearly did not leave myself enough time to answer this question. Please be gentle." My Tax grade did some damage to my overall GPA, and might have kept me from graduating *cum laude*. I still graduated in the top nineteenth percentile, but that last semester break in exam protocol probably cost me those coveted italics. Imagine that your class rank can swing up or down from a little mix-up like this. I was an experienced and skilled test-taker by then, and finding that question with a few minutes remaining was very humbling. I didn't follow the basic protocol of scanning through the entire exam and allocating time for each of the essays. Don't ever let that happen to you.

If, on the other hand, you finish your essay section with time to spare, go back and proofread your work, keeping an eye out for any additional issues you could include. Adding more material can only help your grade; you will only lose points for missing issues or misstating the law, not for being overly verbose or throwing in too many issues. Even if it's simply checking your spelling or grammar, always review your work if time permits.

Unless you have a bathroom emergency, there is absolutely no reason to turn in an exam early and leave the room. If you're given sixty minutes for the exam portion, then use all sixty minutes. I don't care if you're bored or hungry, or if your butt is sore from an uncomfortable chair. If you finish with five or ten minutes to spare, proofread your answers and re-read the fact patterns and questions to see if you spot any new issues or omitted anything. You won't get penalized for saying too much, but you will get penalized for saying too little. Leaving early is the dumbest thing you can do in an essay exam. I recall shaking my head in disbelief as people turned in their exams and left the room with time left on the clock.

The first people to finish exams, despite their smug and confident expressions, are often the ones who miss important issues. They should be taking the time for issue-spotting and proofreading their work, not waltzing out the door. On your exams, there is no award for finishing first.

Proctors

This section is a bit tangential, but it's important.

Your professors will not be present during your exams. It will only be you, your classmates, and the proctors. Exam proctors tend to be local retirees who are getting paid nothing (or close to it) to babysit you during the three to four hours of exam time.

Before every exam begins, a proctor will stand at the podium and read the instructions, which are the same in every exam. Everybody is too anxious to listen to the instructions, of course, and the proctor therefore resembles a flight attendant explaining how to fasten a seatbelt. However unnecessary it may seem, it will behoove you to pay attention to the instructions before the first couple exams so you get a feel for things. You'll definitely want to pay attention if you are taking your exam on a laptop.

Remember, the proctors are donating their time. They're generally pleasant senior citizens trying to support the next generation of lawyers. Don't let your stress rub off on them (or on anybody else, for that matter). Besides the general plus of not being a jerk, you don't want to tick off the person who is in charge of your exam room and could, if they chose, report you for cheating.

Get Your Head Right

While anxiety is inevitable before any exam, it's best to avoid activities that *increase* your anxiety. Your memory and cognition operate optimally when you are rested, calm, collected, and confident. When your blood pressure rises and adrenaline and cortisol kick in, your abilities to think, analyze, and remember are compromised.

For example, if you scan your notes while waiting for an exam to begin, you might start questioning whether you really know the material. By skimming your outline or flashcards, you might confuse yourself in some area where you thought you were secure. This will make you more anxious and erode your confidence. I've experienced this myself, both in exams and in real-life practice.

So, although there will be some downtime before the exam begins, and you might see other students frantically flipping through their notes, try to avoid this temptation. By the time you step into the exam room, you should have done all the reading, prepared your outline, and taken several practice exams. If you haven't done this, a few extra minutes of staring at your outline—especially if you didn't create it yourself—is unlikely to help you. In fact, it's more likely to increase your confusion and anxiety.

My pre-exam routine was to gaze as calmly as possible at some distant, inanimate object while breathing deeply. Sometimes I might close my eyes while doing my deep breathing. This enforced calmness can take practice for some—so if you're prone to nerves, particularly around test-taking, it can be worth it to practice a few meditation and breathing techniques of your choice during the months leading up to exams.

You want to walk into each exam room with the mindset that you have studied as hard as possible and know the material cold. You did the class summaries, you made your own outline, you consulted secondary materials, you made and used your own flashcards, and you took every practice exam you could find; therefore, you are as prepared as it is possible for you to be. I ended my first semester with the sincere belief that I could not have worked harder than I did, and I felt calm and confident during my exams. I walked into the bar exam with the same attitude. People were flipping through notes, and the tension was strong, but I stared straight ahead and focused on my breathing. I brought no notes to distract myself. I'd already done everything I could, and I was as ready as I'd ever be.

This technique of relaxing before big moments helps me in the practice of law as well. I had a trial recently, and found myself anxiously organizing materials on my table and flipping through examination outlines until I suddenly remembered the bar exam. After having a little internal laugh at myself, I put my hands in my lap, focused my vision on a random point ahead of me, and concentrated on my breathing. I did this again in the hallway during a break before resuming a hostile cross-examination that won the case. I felt like I'd activated a superpower.

Before every exam, a proctor will tell you, among other things, to turn off your cell phone. Court personnel always tell lawyers to do the same. This is because phones have a habit of ringing at the worst possible times. My phone is almost always on vibrate mode, but on multiple occasions while arguing in court I have had the uncomfortable and distracting sensation of a cell phone vibrating in my pocket. You don't need this distraction in the exam room any more than you need it in court. Also, outside of life-and-death family situations or other major life circumstances, there is no reason why you need your cell phone with you in the exam room. If you do keep it with you, switch it to airplane mode and leave it in your laptop bag.

If someone nearby has a mental or technical breakdown, you will have to block them out. Even if that person is a friend and your instinct is to help, there is nothing you can do. We're all on our own island. You're not allowed to speak to anyone other than a proctor during an exam. A sympathetic glance is the only support you can provide.

If you have a biological need, like using the restroom, you're better off just getting up and going. Pressure in your bladder will only distract you and cause you to rush your work. I do *not* create my best work when the bathroom is calling. A quick walk up and down the hallway will cost you time, but it could also provide a helpful mental reset.

Finally, you may get distracted by people turning in their exams before you. This can tempt you to question your performance. Don't do that. Keep your head down and finish your exam in your own time. As discussed above, you probably won't want to trade grades with the first people to turn in their exams anyway.

Above all, remember this: while there may be a lot going on inside the exam room, the only person who should matter to you during exam times is you. Incredible focus is required to get through exams. You must be able to shrug off any technical, procedural, emotional, or biological impediments you or those around you may encounter. So, do your breathing or meditation, bring your earplugs (detailed in Chapter 6), and stay as calm as you can so you can do your best work.

That said ...

Whatever Can Go Wrong, Will

From the moment you set foot in the exam room—and, really, from the time you wake up on exam day—you must expect the unexpected. Whatever can go wrong, will, and you will have to adapt.

Expect at least one of the following nightmares to occur at some point during exams in your three years of law school:

- Your laptop battery will die.
- Your computer's hard drive will crash.
- Your pencil's eraser will break off.
- Your mind will go blank. Like, completely blank.
- You will get diarrhea or some other nasty issue right before (or during) an exam.
- You will forget to turn off your cell phone and everyone will shoot you evil death glares.
- You or someone next to you will start crying. Loudly.

None of the above will grant you a second chance at an exam. (Okay, maybe if the diarrhea is bad enough to get you hospitalized, but probably not even then.)

You should also expect heavy traffic on the morning of your exam, no parking spaces, an unusually long line at the coffee cart, or trouble finding the exam location. Give yourself *lots* of extra time—because none of these excuses will fly, either. Supervising partners, judges, and clients don't care about your petty challenges, and neither do law schools. Therefore, you need to be ready to deal with adversity on a level you've never encountered before.

Here's a great example. As I shared in Chapter 7, I took all exams on my laptop. Both schools I attended used software called ExamSoft. During one exam, the program crashed, rendering my computer a frozen, useless, and expensive piece of junk.

I normally have no tolerance for computer glitches. They're one of those petty nuisances in life that just send me to the dark side. But, to my credit (and surprise), I didn't let this get to me during the exam. Instead, I took a deep breath, coolly reached for the written essay booklet they'd given us as a backup, and started writing where I left off. (By the way, I knew to do that because it is among the instructions the proctors gave at the commencement of the exam.)

ExamSoft's autosave feature managed to save most of what I had typed. The IT department of the school was later able to retrieve the pre-crash material, and my professor received both the typed and written portions of my exam. It was no big deal, and I doubt it had any impact on my grade. If I had gotten angry or frustrated, I would have wasted valuable time and mental energy—which *would* have impacted my grade. You can vent your frustration later, and you should, but during the exam you need to compartmentalize and stay composed. You are literally being tested, and sometimes you're tested in unexpected ways.

I didn't just wing those coping skills, though. I learned them by watching a classmate deal with the exact same thing during a mid-term. I don't know whether her computer crashed or the program simply didn't work, but rather than accept her situation and adapt, she tried in vain to plead with a proctor for help. She actually argued a bit and had a little breakdown. Let me tell you, a seventy-something-year-old retiree is not an ideal IT specialist. While the proctor obviously felt sorry for her, there was really nothing he could do except give her an exam booklet (known as a blue book) and suggest that she find her pencil. She wasted valuable minutes rebooting and fussing with her computer, and her frustration definitely impacted her concentration for the rest of the exam. I felt bad for her, but I also learned from her. You will likewise have many opportunities to learn from your classmates' mistakes; make sure you take advantage of them, because—I'll say it again—whatever can go wrong, will.

Avoid "Postmortem" Conversations

When it's all over and you can finally take a breath, it will be very tempting to discuss the exam with your friends. However, you are better off avoiding such "postmortem" conversations. No matter how badly you're dying to know whether people picked (a) or (b) on that Civil Procedure question, and whether they spotted that unenforceable conveyance on the Real Property essay, such conversations provide zero value and can provoke anxiety and "what-if" questions. It might make you feel better to know that others struggled with the same questions as you did, or boost your confidence to know that you breezed through a section where others struggled—but that still doesn't mean it's a good idea to rehash things. You might feel exhilarated to learn that you hit the issues, but your friends will feel the opposite way to hear they *missed* those issues. This will take the wind out of their sails, and they might even resent you, especially if you come across as cocky or relieved. I learned this firsthand after freely discussing exams during my first year. After that, I avoided postmortems like the plague.

During the bar exam, on the day of the multiple-choice section, I went to lunch with some good friends from school at a deli near the exam site. While we waited for our food (and when I had no means of escape), my friends ambushed me with a postmortem. They contradicted me on questions I was sure about, and this subtly eroded my confidence. I responded by changing the subject and stating that I wasn't interested in discussing the exam, period. After that, everything was fine.

If you find yourself in a postmortem social circle, just remove yourself. The exam is out of your hands now, so let it go and move on.

Waiting for Results

Once you turn in your exam, there is nothing more you can do about your grade, so you might as well put it out of your mind.

This might be easier said than done. So, if you think about your exams at all, resolve to think of them in a positive light. Remind yourself that you worked hard, you put in the time and managed your time, you knew the material, you spotted the issues, you avoided distractions, and you are going to return next semester.

The part about being back next semester is true for everyone, as grades might not issue until a third of the way through the following semester. This means you may have invested in new books and materials, completed all the assigned reading, and already started your outlines when you learn you didn't make the cut. The system is pretty cruel, honestly.

I was in the process of moving to a new apartment when my first semester grades were mailed out, and I had redirected my mail to the post office because I didn't want the report card to get delayed by being sent to my old address. I vividly remember walking to the post office counter and receiving a small envelope with four perforated sides. Before walking in, I'd already decided to calmly take the envelope home and read it alone. I didn't know if the results would be good or bad, and I definitely didn't want to be in a public place or the car when I found out.

That was a long drive home; the ten minutes felt like thirty.

I happened to pass my live-in girlfriend a block from home. She pulled up next to me, rolled down her window, and asked, "So ...?"

I coolly responded that I had not yet opened the envelope and drove away, leaving her dumbfounded.

As it turned out, I did far better than I'd expected, and my ranking was in the top 10 percent of my class. This was even more satisfying because, as you'll recall, my low LSAT score caused the school to enroll me in mandatory tutoring.

This leads us to the next topic …

Do Not Rest on Your Laurels

I'm a rabid football fan, but one thing that annoys me about the sport is when athletes become lethargic and unmotivated once they get the big contract. Some athletes lose their motivation to work hard when they become among the highest paid at their position, and it's sad to see such a waste of potential.

After the end of my first semester, I could say with the utmost sincerity that I could not have worked harder than I did, and it showed in my grades and class rank. This probably went to my head a little, because after the second semester I could not truthfully make the same assertion.

Midway through the second semester, I casually mentioned to Professor Stiglitz during office hours (without any context, I'm sure) that I was in the top 10 percent of the first-year class. I was probably just fishing for respect from an intimidating professor. Professor Stiglitz responded that students near the top usually remain at the top.

This comment gave me great comfort. *Too much* comfort. During my second semester, I felt like I was destined for the top of the class, and that my position on the Law Review was manifest destiny; this caused me to take my foot off the gas a bit. While I certainly worked hard my second semester, I could have done much more. As a result, my grades suffered, and my rank fell from the top 10 percent to the top 24 percent.

While 76 percent of the class would have happily changed places with me, it stung to know that I could have stayed in that top-ten position if only my attitude was humbler and hungrier.

Fortunately, that experience humbled me and relit the fire inside me. This helped me in the long run. I transferred to the University of San Diego the following semester, where I studied like my life depended on it. As a result, I graduated with a higher ranking at USD (19 percent) than I had at Cal Western, even though Cal Western was much lower in the school rankings.

The moral of the story is: never let yourself get too comfortable. No one achievement, or set of achievements, will get you a free ticket through law school.

Part IV

Chapter 10

HOW TO SPEND YOUR SUMMER

THE SUMMER BETWEEN my first and second years was bittersweet. I was excited and proud that I not only passed my first year of law school and was about to become an upperclassman, but I had also thrived and vastly exceeded my expectations. While I was confident and cocky, there was also a sense of sorrow that I struggled to honestly acknowledge to myself. Deep down, I felt like I had wasted the opportunity of my positioning after the first semester. I was disappointed because my ranking dropped in the second semester. The prestigious and coveted Law Review was out of reach. I didn't beat myself up, but I knew I was better than my second semester's grades showed, and I had a chip on my shoulder.

I did the best thing I could that summer, and that was to stay active. I accepted an unpaid internship and took two summer school courses. This provided some experience and a few lines in the resume, and I completed two difficult courses that are tested heavily on the bar exam.

You will feel a tremendous sense of relief and accomplishment when your first-year exams are completed. Now, you can look forward to becoming a 2L, and also to look with pity at the new crop of 1Ls coming through the doors.

(Note: From this point forward, I'm going to operate on the assumption that you'll pass your first-year exams and become part of the elite cadre who will continue to become 2Ls. If you don't pass your exams, the rest of this book will be largely irrelevant to you unless you decide to repeat your first year.)

The summer between your first and second years presents you with opportunity and choice. Will you work for money, get an unpaid internship, take summer school, or travel and unwind? Do not make this decision lightly. Unlike in college, you should *not* spend your summer months relaxing at the beach with friends. Nor should you spend them working some temporary gig—unless you need to do so to make ends meet, in which case go ahead and hustle. Instead, you should seek out activities that set you apart from the rest of your class, aka, your future job competitors. If "how did you spend your summer?" is a future interview question (and it may very well be), let your choices be something worth talking about.

Summer School

An obvious option is to get one or two courses out of the way in summer school. This keeps you firmly in your academic process and sets you up for success in the fall semester.

Summer is a good opportunity to get a harder four-unit course out of the way, such as Evidence, because four-unit courses will dominate your study schedule. Also, taking mandatory courses over the summer can help you circumvent the dreaded waitlists. 2Ls are given lower scheduling priority than 3Ls, so taking courses in the summer can prevent you from falling behind later.

In the summer after my first year, before transferring

schools, I took Evidence and Constitutional Law at Cal Western. I figured I could easily get good grades because I only had to focus on two courses. This probably would have worked *if* I had devoted all my time and attention to these two courses, but that wasn't to be.

There were two factors that complicated my summer course success. First, having a full load of classes, like in the regular spring or fall semester, forces you to be a full-time law student. You're on campus all day because you have classes throughout the day. Gaps between classes are spent studying, and you'll likely stay in the library for a couple of hours after classes are done. It's difficult to replicate that if you only have two classes on your schedule. First, you might not have class every day. This is good if you need or want to work part-time, but this also means that you aren't hanging out on campus, where studying is a given. I personally found it hard to have a full-time mindset with a part-time schedule. I thrived better with a full-time courseload than juggling two courses and an internship.

Second, full-time semesters condition you to study during most of your waking hours, and it can be hard to get into a groove like that in the summer, especially in a beach-friendly climate. I found myself barely keeping up with the reading, arriving at campus right before class started, and leaving soon after. My outlines were not exactly a work in progress throughout the summer, but rather thrown together near the end of the semester. Still, I did manage to earn a good, but not great, 84 in Evidence, and a passable but GPA-hurting 78 in Constitutional Law. These grades resulted in a net reduction of my GPA and rank—although I made up for that later.

In summary, if you are the kind of person who can shut out distractions of the weather-related and social varieties, and you're not too burnt out to be effective so soon after exams, summer courses might be a great option for you. This path can also show interviewers that you are dedicated and concerned with getting ahead—both great traits to highlight when seeking a job. You will hit the fall semester with your student mindset and habits already engaged, with extra credits under your belt from courses that your peers are now waitlisted for.

Study Abroad

At some point during your first year, you will inevitably see brochures for a summertime study abroad program. These programs typically involve living in a dormitory-type setting while taking a class that focuses on international legal systems. While actual school credit is provided and it is undoubtedly a lot of fun, everybody knows this is more of an opportunity to travel and party than to study. If you went straight from college to law school without taking a break to backpack around and "find yourself," a study abroad program can be a good excuse to travel and experience a different culture.

One way to determine whether a study abroad program will serve you is to ask yourself, "How likely is it that I will find a practical application for knowledge of international law?" If you're looking at specializing in immigration law, working for the federal government, or working internationally, this experience might actually be useful. On the other hand, it is doubtful that a private civil litigation law firm will be impressed by your summer abroad—although it will certainly earn you more points than sitting around at home. And hey, at least you get school credit.

I never took a summer abroad. I'm sure it's a great time, but I can't really comment on the quality of the experience. I *can* say that, later in my career, when I was in the thick of a heavy litigation practice and conducting interviews for candidate associate attorneys, I never found the study abroad programs very impressive.

Internship and Clerkship

Internships and clerkships are the best way to beef up your resume because they provide you with real-world experience and valuable contacts.

An internship is an unpaid position, usually at a nonprofit or governmental agency. I completely understand if you want or need a paid position, but remember that you will be in a better position to command a wage once you have actual experience under your belt. This is where an internship becomes helpful. Your school's career placement office should have ample resources for you to explore internship opportunities.

During the summer after my first year, I interned for the Utility Consumer Action Network (UCAN), a nonprofit utility watchdog group, while taking my two courses. I found this opportunity through an opening listed at my school's career office.

This was my first interview, and when I sat down with the founder, I opened with the most idiotic statement imaginable: "Tell me about UCAN's mission." The founder's face puckered like he'd bitten into a lemon. He incredulously responded, "Shouldn't you already know that?" The sad thing was I already was familiar with UCAN's mission. I was naively trying to open the interview with a conversational tone. I unwittingly made myself appear totally unprepared and ignorant. It also conveyed hubris, as if I was interviewing him, not the other way around.

Normal job interviews are somewhat of a two-way affair, but internships are not. Regardless of your grades and aptitudes, you are a lowly student with no legal experience. Know your place. Thankfully, I recovered from that rocky start and still managed to get the internship. (It is also possible that UCAN had no other applicants—I have no way of knowing.)

My internship with UCAN was a good experience overall. It gave me a writing sample, a little experience, something to put on my resume, and a lot of confidence.

I attended a job fair at UCLA before my second year ended. I signed up in advance to interview with a state agency, figuring my previous summer with UCAN would give me a leg up. I donned my only suit and drove two hours to Los Angeles. The woman conducting the interview was very apathetic about being there, and candidly disclosed that the agency had decided against hiring any interns that summer. She said UCLA asked the agency to attend anyway because so few employers were participating in the event. The day seemed like a total waste of time, but instead of going home angry, I decided to walk through the job fair and see who was there. I'd had enough foresight to bring some resumes, and chatted with a representative from San Diego Coastkeeper, a nonprofit clean water advocacy group. I was interested in environmental law, and this led to an unpaid internship with Coastkeeper. I got to work with several of my classmates and made some new friends.

While interning with Coastkeeper, I also clerked at a real estate litigation firm. The pay was slightly less than I made as a line cook, but that didn't matter—I was getting real experience at a real firm. I started out working the phones at the reception desk. That wasn't exactly a fun position, and I accidentally hung up on a few people because the phone system was confusing. After a few days of enduring reception, my job duties changed to legal research and memoranda, something I'd actually learned in school. However, working reception for those few days helped me learn the mechanics of how a law office is run, and I developed a healthy respect for the roles of legal staff.

After these experiences, the big picture started coming together for me as a 3L. Thanks to my summer gigs, I saw that what we were learning in school had real-life applications. This helped me ask more focused and real-world questions as a 3L.

Judicial clerkships, where you assist a judge behind the scenes and watch the action in court, are the most coveted positions. Those look great on a resume. I never had a judicial clerkship, but given my current career as a litigator, it would have been incredibly valuable. Keep your eyes open for any judicial clerkship opportunities. I would advise you to choose a clerkship over a summer internship at a big law firm.

Regardless of whether you find a volunteer internship or a paid clerkship, actual work experience looks the best on your resume and can lead to important references and contacts. Therefore, I strongly advise you to consider interning or clerking during the summer after your first year, especially in a field that relates to the type of work you want to do later.

Remember to Have Fun

Having filled your head with all the activities you could and should be doing, I want to remind you to also carve out some time to rest and recharge (whatever that means for you). I'll avoid the word "balance" because that's something that eludes most professionals—but please try to spend time with family and friends, binge watch some great shows, meditate, nurture your hobbies, exercise, play sports, attend concerts, etc. Staying in touch with yourself and minding your self-care and happiness is critical. None of this hard work will mean much, and the education will be less rewarding, if you sacrifice relationships and your happiness in pursuit of a law degree.

If you don't take some time to rest and recharge, you will burn out and rebel against the course material. This will compound your stress and make you very unhappy. This advice is equally applicable during the semester as it is between semesters, but you might find more opportunities to explore different things in the winter and summer breaks. Sometimes you need to put down the book and turn off the computer.

This advice applies equally to life after law school, so it's best to develop good habits now, rather than try to build them in when you're meeting the demands of life as a lawyer. You're no good to anyone if you're burnt out and unhappy, and your studies will suffer, so don't forget to take care of yourself.

Chapter 11

YOUR SECOND AND THIRD YEARS

MY FIRST-YEAR Contracts professor taught with a PowerPoint presentation and handout. The questions *and* answers were all on the handout and on a projector screen for the whole class to follow.

This professor was rather easygoing—definitely not one of the deliberate intimidators—and he was asking questions with the answer literally written in lights above his head on the projector screen. Somehow, certain students just weren't catching on, and they struggled to answer his questions.

My friends and I snickered at the absurdity, directing unwanted attention to ourselves, which caused the professor to call on me. I answered his question by reading from the projector screen, word for word, bobbing my head with each syllable for emphasis, like one of those bouncing ball commercials from the 80s. This was my arrogant and inartful way of signaling to the professor that we weren't really learning because we didn't have to think. (Yes, I was an immature smartass. I've mellowed a bit since then—but only a bit.)

Some of my classmates thought the incident was funny. Others were appalled. After class, a small mob of students sought me out, determined to chastise me for my insubordination. Fortunately, they confused me with another Tom in the class, and he absorbed the sneers of the pitchfork-wielding mob for me.

My Criminal Law class was taught in Cal Western's moot courtroom—a grand, ornate room with wood paneling that provides excellent acoustics. I sat near several friends, and during one lecture was entertaining them by making realistic-sounding fart sounds under the desk with my cupped hands. (Immature smartass, remember?) The professor was speaking through the PA system, and his voice easily drowned me out—or so I thought.

I was happily ripping away when the professor paused to sip his coffee. As it turned out, the professor probably didn't need the PA system, because the acoustics in that room were so excellent that my under-desk soundtrack filled the entire room. My face turned white with horror as the entire class of about 100 students honed their sonar systems to the source of the sound.

I looked to my right to avoid eye contact with the professor, only to find two rows of red-faced students grunting with suppressed laughter. It was like we were back in third grade.

However, teenage antics weren't the only way I embarrassed myself as a law student.

Don't Take Yourself So Seriously

In my first year, my love for public speaking caused me to speak out often with questions and commentary.

I became aware of this propensity during the second semester of my Real Property class. The professor was discussing issues relating to ancillary structures on a property. Thoughts and questions were bouncing around my head faster than I could process them, and I reflexively raised my hand. "What about chicken coops? What about doghouses?" I spoke so fast that my mouth could barely keep pace with my brain.

The professor shut me down and barked, "STOP! I'm not getting into Sparky the dog."

It was a bit of a slap in the face, but I needed it. I was so intensely focused on the material that I lost the forest for the trees. I then had to deal with the fallout from my classmates, some of whom mockingly called me "Sparky."

The moral of the story is, if you don't learn to keep yourself in check, you will be in for a world of hurt. Take your studies seriously, but don't take *yourself* too seriously.

Now that you've made the cut, it's tempting to think you know everything about law school and how to survive it. You now know that the professors will pick you apart, that your future career seems to hinge on every word you speak in class, and that there will be days when you can't seem to remember your own name, let alone the Rule Against Perpetuities.

A student's role is to be hardworking, inquisitive, resourceful, and respectful of the process. It can be tempting to think that, since you survived Year One, that you are somehow beyond that. Your professors will soon disabuse you of that notion.

To succeed in your second and third years, you need to keep things in perspective. After all, you are still only a law student. You haven't graduated, you haven't passed the bar exam, and you haven't practiced law. Regardless of your scholastic achievements, you haven't accomplished anything in your legal career beyond your first-year grades and whatever you did last summer. You're still a newbie, and you should remember that.

Some law students forget they're not actually lawyers yet and assume an air of self-importance. High rankings, internships, and scholarships, in particular, can do this to people. I once chatted with a school acquaintance about his experience clerking at a firm. He talked about a strategy session with the lawyers on a case, and how a *secretary* volunteered an opinion. My acquaintance clearly believed that a lowly legal secretary had no business discussing the merits of a case. His attitude was straight out of *Mad Men*. This guy utterly failed to appreciate that, as a 1L law clerk, the secretary was actually above him on the firm's totem pole of seniority and respect. Moreover, no one—student or fully-fledged lawyer—should ever presume that the opinions of clerical staff are worthless. We can *always* benefit from the perspective of educated laypeople.

When you get your license, everyone at the law firm, including all staff, will literally have more legal experience than you. You should conduct yourself accordingly, and this applies even more when you're clerking at a firm as a student.

Now, let me tell you about that time when I smuggled a bag of CornNuts into the library.

For obvious reasons, libraries generally don't allow eating and drinking. Still, I was feeling peckish, and I'd chosen a quiet and remote cubicle down in the basement, where I was less likely to be disturbed (or spotted).

Eager to enjoy my tasty contraband, I popped one solitary CornNut into my mouth. Somewhere after the first crunch and before the second, a female student popped out of an adjacent cubicle, got right in my face, and loudly stammered, "Please, no eating … CornNuts … in the library!" She then vanished as quickly as she'd appeared.

I was flabbergasted. The whole event seemed surreal; after several seconds of stupefied silence, the only response I could muster was, "Are you for real?"

"Yes, I am," she snapped.

However, while I applauded her catlike hearing, reflexes,

and agility, she was like a rubber band stretched too far. To be fair, CornNuts are probably the loudest and smelliest snack food a person can eat, and I *was* breaking the no food rule, but her reaction seemed extreme. It then dawned on me that finals were approaching, and (after a surreptitious peek over the cubicle wall) I saw that she had a Corporations casebook on her desk. Corporations is one of the more intensive courses in law school, and this woman was not about to let my CornNuts get between her and her dreams.

Lesson One: don't eat in the library.

Lesson Two: if you are going to eat in the library, smuggle something quieter than CornNuts.

Lesson Three: if you find yourself ready to flip out on a total stranger over the slightest disruption to your study session, that's an indication that you need to step away, relax, and regain some perspective. Not only are you a menace to everyone in your vicinity, you are not in a good state of mind to retain material or think clearly.

Don't be the CornNut lady. Life is too short.

Also, don't be like me. Respect your fellow students.

Choosing Your Courses

As a 1L, you have no say in the courses you take. Every course is predetermined and there is nothing you can do about it.

Life as a 2L and 3L is more like college. Your school will require certain courses in order to obtain the degree, and you will be provided with a selection of electives. As I mentioned in Chapter 10, course selection is a bit harder as a 2L because 3Ls are given scheduling priority. You might get waitlisted on your favored courses, so you should have backups in mind.

TIP #1: TAKE COURSES THAT ARE TESTED ON THE BAR EXAM

Bar examiners always focus heavily on certain subject matter, including all first-year courses plus Evidence, Constitutional Law, and Criminal Procedure. Other subjects are rotated in and out of the exam.

Some courses, like Evidence and Constitutional Law, are required to get your degree. Other bar courses, such as Trusts and Estates and UCC Sales, are elective. Some schools require students to take courses that are not tested on the bar. (For example, Tax is a required course at USD but is not tested on the bar exam.)

Obviously, taking bar exam courses will help you pass the bar, and bar exam electives should be a priority regardless of your desired practice area.

I got carried away with non-bar exam electives and should have taken more bar courses than I actually did. I made up for this by taking a bar review course immediately after graduation. The class provided a crash-course summary of every subject tested on the bar exam. This was the first time I really learned anything about subjects like Community Property and Wills and Trusts. It was stressful to learn subjects for the first time while studying for the bar exam. I felt like I was totally behind the eight-ball compared to my classmates.

That said, while it is important to have some background with subjects tested on the bar, you shouldn't use *all* your electives on bar exam courses. Instead, take advantage of this opportunity to see what else is available and explore your interests. You just might discover an area of the law you never considered.

TIP #2: TAKE CLASSES THAT ARE RELEVANT TO YOUR JURISDICTION

If you attend school in the state where you intend to practice law, I highly recommend taking courses that are relevant to your jurisdiction. Law school is generally about theory, not practice. A course like Real Property, for example, teaches you about the evolution of property principles from medieval England to the present, and you will read cases from across the country. But if you intend to practice law in Nevada, cases you've read from Maryland won't help you much.

The law varies from state to state. While the laws among certain states can be very similar, they can also fluctuate dramatically. It's great that you know the majority of states follow Rule X, while the minority of states follow Rule Y, but what rule does your state follow? When you pass the bar and start practicing in the real world, the only thing that matters is the law in the state where you practice.

Civil Procedure is a required course for all first-year students. This course teaches you how to practice in federal court. While many of the concepts are applicable in state court, and many states enact codes that resemble the Federal Rules of Civil Procedure, you will need to learn how to practice in your given state. Even if you practice solely in federal court, state law governs the action in certain cases. Plus, every federal district has its own local rules and customs. USD offers a course called California Civil Procedure, where I learned concepts I frequently apply in practice today. This was one of the more useful courses I took in my three years of school, as I knew I wanted to be a civil litigator in California.

You can hit the ground running and make yourself more appealing to prospective employers by demonstrating practical knowledge about the law in your home state. Such courses won't necessarily help you pass the bar, but they will provide real-world, practical knowledge you can actually use.

TIP #3: TAKE CLASSES THAT ARE RELEVANT TO YOUR CHOSEN PRACTICE AREA

Electives are a great opportunity to delve into a specialty and explore different areas of the law to learn where your interests lie. I realized civil litigation was for me sometime during my summer of clerking at a law firm. I had no desire to practice criminal law, but I knew I wanted to be in court. I therefore took electives that related to civil litigation, and many of those courses helped me immensely in practice. That said, with the benefit of hindsight, there are many subjects I regret missing.

I'm Glad I Took These Courses

You won't choose a "major" in law school, but you should definitely take courses that complement and build upon each other. My goal was to take courses that made me a well-rounded civil litigator. In addition to first-year Civil Procedure, I took multiple upper-class courses that focused on civil procedure in state and federal court.

Administrative Law was one of the more useful courses. While it definitely wasn't a sexy subject, it has massive practical application. This course teaches how government agencies function, including municipalities and state licensing agencies. I apply what I learned in this course all the time, including public record research, subpoenaing government agencies, deposing government employees, and researching the validity of professional licenses.

I've been on many cases involving disputes between private

litigants where some governmental agency is involved on some level, usually licensing or permitting. To be successful in such cases, you need some understanding of how government agencies work, their potential role(s) in your case, and how to extract information from these agencies. I've been on many cases where a party or witness has (or claims to have) a professional license, and it is very useful to know how to research the validity or status of that person's license. If nothing else, Administrative Law makes you more resourceful.

Bankruptcy was also a surprisingly relevant course. Every civil litigator will have plenty of cases that end up in bankruptcy court. The regular rules of civil procedure do not apply, and everything is governed by federal bankruptcy statutes (although discovery rules from the FRCP do apply). Even if you don't practice bankruptcy law and never appear in bankruptcy court, at some point you will find yourself counseling a client about whether filing bankruptcy is an option, or whether the dischargeability of a debt is worth fighting over in bankruptcy court. Even if you refer the client to a bankruptcy specialist (which I recommend and frequently do), you will provide value by spotting and analyzing bankruptcy issues. While I don't practice bankruptcy law myself, I know enough to advise certain clients to seek bankruptcy consultations so they can weigh their options.

I had a contentious federal copyright case in San Diego where one defendant filed bankruptcy in Missouri. This guy probably thought he'd found a way out of the lawsuit by seeking bankruptcy protection thousands of miles away. I retained a local bankruptcy specialist in Missouri to help navigate us through the local bankruptcy process while my firm managed the objectives. Having some background in bankruptcy from law school helped me understand the core concepts, and this enabled me to work effectively with local counsel.

I took Cyberspace Law on a whim. Remember, this was the early 2000s, when state and federal legislatures were just starting to pass laws governing the internet. The law is always years behind technology, and Internet Law is fascinating because the law seldom matches perfectly to the facts of a case (although in this area it has since caught up considerably). This leaves room for creative lawyering. At some point every civil litigator will encounter a client or opponent who did or said something stupid online, creating real-world repercussions. Today, with internet platforms being the primary medium for social interactions and commercial transactions, "digital law" is not just a nice-to-have but a necessity in many, if not most, areas of legal practice. If your school offers any kind of Cyberspace or Internet Law course, you need to sign up.

I took Labor Law out of pure curiosity, and learned that I had no interest in representing unions or management. The subject matter did nothing for me, and I've never applied anything I learned in that course. It's okay to take a course that turns out to be useless, as long as it doesn't hurt your GPA. Sometimes you have to date the wrong person to learn what you don't want in a partner.

I Regret Missing These Courses

Looking back, it would have been helpful to have some foundation in employment law. My first employment case came several years into my career, when I represented a high-profile employer. I had to learn the law on the fly, and much of my time learning basic employment law had to be written off, meaning my firm lost money on the time I spent researching. (Side note: clients are paying you to advise them and work their cases, not to teach yourself something you should already know.) Some of the discovery I served in that case was admittedly off the mark, and the plaintiff's counsel must have thought he was up against a total incompetent. I eventually got my act together and got the case dismissed on a motion for summary judgment. While we got the best possible result for our client, and it *was* my first ever employment case, I spun my wheels pursuing non-issues because I didn't know the law. I felt a bit more comfortable with the next employment case that came along, but I still wish I'd taken Employment Law in school.

Another course I regret missing is Trusts and Estates. Not only is this course tested on the bar exam (and, as such, I had to learn it by the seat of my pants in the bar review course after graduation), but it is also extremely important. I briefly worked at a probate litigation firm and learned just enough to understand how little I know about estate planning and probate. Unless you live in a cave, at some point in your career, someone you know, or a friend or relative of someone you know, is going to need an estate plan, or may die with or without one. You don't necessarily have to take on cases like this, but it is helpful to have enough knowledge of estate planning and probate law to provide basic guidance.

I once inherited a federal case in Arizona, receiving the file *after* the trial was already done, but the judge wanted additional briefing on legal issues. One of the defendants died shortly before trial, and the legal effect of her passing became a major issue in the case. My predecessor knew about the death but instead of researching the ramifications, he just plowed ahead as if nothing had happened. My brief time with the probate firm helped me spot issues in the case, and I did my best to contain the damage of my predecessor's oversight. However, a strong foundation on the subject matter in school would have helped.

Another reason to take Trusts and Estates is the personal

benefit to you and your family. Estate planning is an important component of getting your financial house in order, along with retirement planning. A background in Trusts and Estates could potentially save you thousands in legal fees because you can prepare your own estate plan.

Lastly, I wish I had taken a course in Land Use. If you want to build an apartment complex or office building, you can't just buy the land and show up with shovels. Land developers must go through a lengthy and expensive entitlement process with many government agencies. In order to get the many permits required to commence construction, you will need to petition several agencies with engineer-created plans, which requires public hearings. I've had more cases than I can count where the land entitlement process was an important issue. I had to learn the process on the fly through online research and by picking the brains of my clients and experts. Again, a scholastic foundation in Land Use would have been of great benefit.

I'm Glad I Didn't Waste My Time on These Courses

I was a Philosophy major, so I'm not one to knock academic courses like Philosophy of Law or Jurisprudence, but unlike college, you are in a vocational school now, and you are training for a profession. Plenty of bar courses delve deep into history, philosophy, and theory, and your priority should be courses that prepare you for the actual practice of law. If you want to go into a career of education, academia, and writing, then by all means take courses like those mentioned above. If you want to be a practicing attorney, I advise you to take more practical courses.

TIP #4: EXPAND YOUR HORIZONS (AND DON'T PIGEONHOLE YOURSELF)

Law school is a great opportunity to explore your interests with electives that spark your curiosity. If a practice area intrigues you and your school offers a relevant elective, then by all means sign up and/or sit in on some classes. I took an Environmental Law course and transferred out after attending a few classes. While I like to think of myself as an environmentalist, I came off the waitlist in another course I needed for graduation, and my gut told me to transfer out.

If you deliberately take courses that spark your curiosity, they aren't all going to be winners, but that doesn't mean you should play it safe. This is the time to expand your horizons and see what speaks to you.

I took a Labor Law course because the Employment Law course was full, but I didn't understand the difference between the two. I quickly discovered that the subject matter didn't interest me very much, but I rode out the semester because I liked the professor. I've never worked in that area of the law and the course ultimately has not been useful in my career, but I enjoyed the course and have no regrets.

TIP #5: TAKE PRACTICUM COURSES TO GET ACTUAL EXPERIENCE

USD has a vibrant legal clinic program where students get provisionally licensed by the State Bar to practice law under the supervision of a professor, and it has a variety of clinics in different areas. There is a civil litigation clinic, a family law clinic, an employment clinic, and several others.

I took the Civil Clinic for two semesters. This clinic provides legal services to indigent clients who qualify under the income threshold. The clinic itself and the supervising attorney served as the attorney of record, and I was able to sign documents and appear in court. The caseload was distributed among the students and we were often paired together on cases. The clinic had resources just like a law firm, including a paralegal. I got some helpful courtroom and deposition experience. It also led to a clerkship with my professor, and I later became his associate and started my career at his firm.

If your school has a clinic program, or any other way for you to get real-world experience, then this elective must be a priority.

And Finally, Keep Your Nose Clean

Back in my days as a line cook, I worked under a chef who was a graduate of the California Culinary Academy in San Francisco. He said the competition was so fierce that students would furtively alter the temperature on others' stovetops, causing a sauce to unexpectedly burn.

Around the same time, I heard an urban legend about hyper-competitive law students who defaced books in the library so their classmates could not read the material. I laughed at this then—surely lawyers weren't as hot-headed as chefs!

I never saw defaced books, so this fortunately was not my experience. However, I did discover that people are capable of terrible things, especially when grades and livelihoods are at stake, and this dynamic is enhanced when ultra-competitive people are placed in an ultra-competitive environment like law school (or real-life law practice).

No matter how much you want to edge out the competition, don't be that person. Never compromise yourself by doing something dishonest or unethical in order to gain an actual or perceived advantage. If you succeed in life, it should be because of your talent, intelligence, and work ethic, not because you know how to manipulate the system or your peers. This is even more true in practice. Even if being underhanded provides an immediate or short-term benefit, your deeds will catch up to you. Lawyers especially need to keep their noses clean, and this equally includes future lawyers in law school.

Someone who is willing to break the rules in school will also be willing to break the rules as a licensed attorney. If you've already crossed the line and engaged in shady behavior as a student—and by "shady" I mean doing stuff like cheating on exams or sabotaging other students, not sneaking CornNuts into the library—you're on the path to becoming a shady lawyer. The State Bar knows this. California requires prospective licensees to pass a "moral character exam," which includes the Model Professional Responsibility Exam and a background check. Every agency regulating the practice of law in every state issues its own Rules of Professional Conduct, which provide some guidance for ethical problems that commonly arise. Violation of these rules can cost you your law license, temporarily or permanently.

The State Bar also looks into your background to determine whether there are any red flags suggesting a history of "moral turpitude." In short, the State Bar is looking to weed out people who might steal from their clients or otherwise harm the public or impugn the reputation of the legal profession as a whole. The State Bar's mission, on paper, is to protect the public, but it also serves the profession. The State Bar will look into your criminal record, but it will forgive youthful indiscretions such as drunk in public or minor in possession of alcohol (if you were the minor, not the person giving alcohol to the minor). Any lawsuits you have been party to are also fair game. The State Bar will examine your collegiate file to see if you got into any trouble at school. It will request non-familial references and also pull your credit report. It will look unfavorably upon you if you were suspended at any point for cheating, stalking, or harassing. It will also look unfavorably upon poor financial management. Bankruptcies and poor credit are not indicative of moral turpitude, but neither is a checkered credit history indicative of someone who should be handling client funds.

The process of demonstrating moral fortitude feels like you are an FBI applicant going through a security screening. However, every time you walk into court, you function as an "officer of the court." The State Bar exists to ensure that this title isn't bestowed upon just anybody. You should take this seriously in practice, but it begins in school.

If you intend to become a lawyer in any state, you will have to pass the background check. You therefore must keep your nose clean and be honest with the State Bar investigators. Being evasive when being asked directly about your indiscretions could jeopardize your ability to get a bar license, regardless of your bar exam score. As Richard Nixon taught us, sometimes the cover up is worse than the crime.

Everyone has some kind of skeleton in their closet. We all have some youthful indiscretions we wish never happened, but our indiscretions are part of our identities, and experience is an invaluable teacher. The State Bar doesn't care about most of your indiscretions; rather, it wants to see if you are *forthcoming* about them. If you have been suspended from school for any reason, you must disclose it when the question is asked. I had a little too much fun in the dorms my freshman year of college, and was suspended for a semester for non-academic reasons. I therefore had to check the "Yes" box when the question came up on the form, but I had an opportunity to explain the circumstances on a separate page. I knew a piece of paper existed at my alma mater that detailed the terms of my suspension because I had a copy of that paper. I assumed the State Bar would receive a copy of this letter and that I couldn't hide from this incident. In drafting my explanation to the State Bar, I avoided writing a narrative about my former partying habits. I simply quoted from the university letter. I disclosed the incident exactly as the university had it documented. I was truthful but did not volunteer any information beyond what was contained in the letter. Aside from that incident, I avoided getting into any significant trouble throughout college and law school, and so the incident didn't stop me from becoming licensed in California.

All of us have an edge. When we are pushed to it, we can do things we wouldn't ordinarily consider. You will likely meet this edge in law school. You may find yourself thinking thoughts and acting in ways that would be anathema to you under normal circumstances. In fact, I'm pretty sure that CornNut Lady was a kind and patient person when she wasn't cramming for exams.

In the end, it's not about what you think, but what you do. If you are willing to cross the line and engage in unethical behavior, no matter the justification, you have no place in the legal profession. The biggest asset an attorney has is their reputation—and it could take years to repair a tarnished reputation. The foundations of your reputation begin in law school and will either support or undermine you for your entire career. So, do the right thing, and you'll have no regrets.

Chapter 12

TRANSFERS

I SPENT A YEAR and a half at a fourth-tier school and two years at a second-tier school, and can honestly say that neither school was better than the other. I had good and bad professors at each school, and both had pluses and minuses. Ultimately, I'm satisfied with my decision to transfer because my degree from my chosen school carries more weight, and it gave me a leg up in the local job hunt. This matters less the further into your career you are, but the school you graduate from is *very* important early in your career.

As I've shared, despite my poor LSAT score and initial rejection by USD, I graduated with a higher rank at USD than I had at Cal Western. For that reason, I don't put a lot of stock into the LSAT score. Unfortunately, law schools do.

Why Transfer?

If an opportunity to transfer schools presents itself and the prospective school is ranked higher than your current school, you should seriously consider transferring—as long as you aren't tied down with a scholarship. As I stated earlier, a scholarship that is conditional upon finishing your degree at that school is a heavy deterrent against transferring. This chapter is therefore directed at those who do not have a scholarship.

As I've shared, USD rejected me when I applied the first time during my final semester in college. This was not a big surprise because of my grades and LSAT. However, I was accepted as a transfer student after a solid first year at Cal Western. The Director of Admissions at USD told me they happily take students from Cal Western because they know it is a good school.

Even if you don't get accepted to the school of your choice, the possibility of transferring after a stellar first year should keep you motivated, and solid first-year grades can propel you to a school that denied you the year before. This makes sense because a high ranking proves that you know how to succeed in law school, and this will help you overcome poor undergraduate grades or a low LSAT.

I never considered transferring during my first year at Cal Western. I was totally focused on getting good grades and wasn't interested in looking elsewhere. (Note: you can't transfer without the grades, so put in the work!) After enrolling in summer classes, I heard a rumor—a law school "urban myth," if you will—that if Cal Western knew you were applying for a transfer and you had halfway decent grades, you might be offered a scholarship as an incentive to stay put.

I figured that, if this were true, applying for a transfer to USD could serve me either way and I had nothing to lose. As the application deadline at USD was quickly approaching, I impulsively fired off an application and hoped for the best, without any attachment to the outcome. I was perfectly fine staying put—but if you don't ask, the answer is always "no," so it was worth a try.

While applying for the transfer I had to direct the admissions office at Cal Western to send my transcript to USD. I assumed this might trigger a review or red flag and that Cal Western would try to retain me. I have no idea whether such a system was or is in place; I can only say that Cal Western made no effort to stop me from transferring. It felt like the school called my bluff, since my goal at the time was to leverage a scholarship, not to actually transfer. Either way, it worked out: USD accepted my application, and I accepted the invitation because a degree from USD would carry more weight in the local job market and tuition was about the same.

Should You Transfer?

You should consider transferring if you had a solid first year and are anywhere in the top half of your class. Ideally, you will only transfer if the new school has a higher ranking which could enhance your employment prospects, or there is some other career-related benefit at play. I do *not* recommend transferring to follow a girlfriend or boyfriend, or because another campus is in a nicer city or has better facilities. Those benefits are secondary and may not outweigh the downsides of a transfer.

You might be tempted to transfer so you can be closer to family, especially if someone needs your help. If a family crisis emerges and you need to be a caregiver, this will impede your ability to be an effective student. Rather than a transfer, I would suggest a leave of absence. Moving and changing schools, in addition to the family emergency, will hurt your grades and employment prospects, whereas if you pause schooling to deal with your family situation first, then return to school when you're better able to focus on your studies, you will run less risk of slipping in the rankings.

Unless a prospective school is offering you a scholarship, transferring to a lower-ranked school is self-defeating and should not be considered. If a lower-tiered school offered you a scholarship, you would have to weigh whether the short-term savings in tuition would offset the reduced income you might receive for the first decade of your career. In most cases, I would advise you to stay put and pay the full tuition at a higher-ranked school.

Transferring Isn't Always Linear

One potential difficulty with transferring schools is that different schools have different graduation requirements. USD's first-year curriculum was slightly different than Cal Western, and as a 2L at USD I had to retake a semester of first-year Torts and Lawyering Skills with the 1Ls. This made me feel like I was a remedial student, the older kid who got held back a year. I'm sure my 1L classmates also wondered why a 2L transfer student was in their class. I heard audible snickers and scoffing anytime I was called on in class. Fortunately, I had already taken Torts at Cal Western and earned an excellent grade, so I just kept my mouth shut and did the work. I got an A in both classes and refused to let the immaturity of others knock me off course.

The Lawyering Skills course got off to a rough start. The professor was quite critical of my first writing assignment, and when I visited her during office hours to ask why my paper was practically dipped in red ink, she adopted a tone of "I don't know how they taught you to write at Cal Western, but here at USD ..." The professor constantly called on me in class and I got the distinct impression she was harder on me *because* I was a 2L—that I was being held to a higher standard. I couldn't fight her, so I just worked harder. Unlike at Cal Western, the Lawyering Skills course at USD did not provide a letter grade. This was a pass/fail course, with honors given to a select few. I got the honors.

If you are forced to take or repeat a 1L course as a 2L due to a transfer, be prepared for the possibility that your classmates and professors might treat you differently at first. While it's tempting to see this as an unwelcome distraction and added pressure, consider it added motivation for you to stay focused on your studies—and also a potential gift to your GPA. I personally used the attitude I saw around me as rocket fuel to leap ahead of my classmates in the rankings—which those two high grades helped me do.

The Social Equation

Some of the disadvantages of transferring are obvious but temporary. For example, you will have to get acclimated to a new campus, figure out where to park, where to eat, where to spend downtime, etc. I only mention this because these inconveniences can lead to missed classes and less study time unless you give yourself extra time to get accustomed to your new routines.

Since I transferred within the same city, there were only a few logistical hiccups for me. My biggest challenge by far was on the social front.

The first year of law school is an intense experience, and as such creates a level of bonding I had not experienced elsewhere. Everybody knows everybody by the time the year is over, and such tight-knit cliques can be tough to crack as an outsider.

The experience reminds me of an episode of *Band of Brothers* called "The Replacements," where fresh reinforcements were integrated with those who survived D-Day. It took them some time to be accepted—assuming they survived. Arriving at a new school as a 2L felt much the same.

While the students at USD endured the same experiences in their first year that I did at Cal Western, and I knew exactly what they'd gone through, I didn't go through it *with them*. During my first semester as a 2L, I got the distinct sense that I was being watched under a microscope by my classmates—a "Who is this transfer guy?" vibe. This caused me to keep a bit of a low profile. I was extroverted and talkative in class as a 1L, but as a 2L I felt like I had to hold back to avoid being attacked. This forced me to outgrow the bombastic attitude I exhibited as a 1L, and probably served me in the long run.

Another difference I noted after the transfer was the general attitude of the students on campus. Throughout my two years at USD, I noticed that many students had more of a pompous and privileged attitude than at Cal Western. When somebody spoke in class, I often noticed eye rolls, sighs, giggles, murmurs, and hissing. This was discouraging because it probably chilled a lot of the voluntary participation in class, and everyone loses when that happens. I believe the competition was more intense at USD because students were more invested in their education and their resumes; they took themselves more seriously. I don't mean to imply that students at Cal Western—or at any third- or fourth-tier school—do not work hard and are not extremely bright people. However, I believe students at lower-tiered schools are thankful to be attending law school in the first place and don't tend to waste their energy by pretending they are better than others. At Cal Western, it felt like everybody was judging and evaluating everyone else, but it never felt nasty or elitist. In contrast, the intensity level at USD was ratcheted *way* up, and this magnified the feeling of being an outsider.

Jessica, a student from Cal Western, transferred to USD at the same time as me. While we weren't particularly close, we were comforting and familiar faces to each other in a new and intimidating environment. Jessica had a rather raspy voice. In one class at USD while Jessica was responding to a professor's questions, I overheard a clique of students referring to her as "party girl" because of her voice. They gossiped about how she was a transfer student, and their tone implied that she was not worthy of being in their presence. I took great offense, not only on Jessica's behalf, but because they were also indirectly describing me.

If you are accepted as a transfer student to a first- or second-tier school, remember that the more highly ranked the school, the higher the undergraduate GPA and LSAT scores of the student body. Students at top-ranked schools have worked incredibly hard to get there, and they might be hostile to someone transferring from a lower-tiered school. Ignore them. You enrolled in school to advance your own career, not to win a popularity contest. And you obviously *do* belong there, because you were accepted.

***

In summary, if you didn't get accepted to your dream school, you performed well in your first year, and if you are unencumbered by a scholarship, then transferring is a viable path to acceptance at a school that was out of reach before. Hopefully this chapter has given you a lot to consider, but it never hurts to submit a transfer application and explore your options.

Part V

Chapter 13

THE BAR AND BEYOND

YOU DID IT, MY FRIEND.

You rented a cap and gown. You walked across the stage at the graduation ceremony with family, friends, and classmates cheering you on. You posed for the obligatory photos, then attended a special dinner with your loved ones.

You graduated from law school, and regardless of your grades and rank, this is an accomplishment you can be proud of forever. You now have the degree of *Juris Doctor* and can use the "JD" designation after your name, signifying that you are a graduate of law school.

Your loved ones will brag about you. Your non-lawyer friends will breathe a sigh of relief, knowing you won't be bringing casebooks to the pub on Saturday nights. You and all those close to you can breathe a sigh of relief. The worst is over.

Or is it?

It can be tempting to slack off and celebrate—and you certainly should, for a few days. But after that, you'll want to put yourself back in your studious mindset, because your biggest battle and final rite of passage is still ahead.

Yes, my friend. It's time to prepare for the bar exam—the one hurdle still standing between you and your license to practice law.

My Bar Exam Experience

Your first crack at the bar exam is critical because first-time bar exam-takers have the highest chance of success. While plenty of attorneys overcome a bad first test to pass and become licensed on their second, third, or even fourth attempt, statistics show that your chance of passing the bar drops with every subsequent attempt. Don't give up if you fail, or even if you fail multiple times—but don't bank on second chances, either. Make your first time count.

I'm going to be real with you. I did pass the bar on my first attempt, but I did so *despite* some of my most prominent study habits, not because of them. You've come this far with me, so I owe it to you to speak the truth: while I have some solid advice that will serve you well, you should also treat this next section as primer on how *not* to prepare for the bar exam.

The summer of 2003 was a time of much personal change and transformation for me. I ended my relationship with my long-term, live-in girlfriend a couple of months before graduation and moved into a one-bedroom apartment in Pacific Beach. This party-town location was great for people like me: single, twenty-something, and out to have fun. My priorities reflected my level of maturity. I attended the bar review course by day, and went out on dates at night. I discovered internet dating when it was still websites and emails.

I vividly recall one of the speakers at the bar review course who spoke to us about study habits and lifestyle. "No matter what your vices were during law school," he told the class, "do whatever worked for you then, and don't change anything now." Giggles were audible throughout the auditorium. I personally may have taken this as permission to spend my evenings at bars and clubs with my internet dates—but overall, it was wise advice. All of us had gotten through law school despite our habits and vices; to try to change those before the bar exam would be too stressful and likely work against us. Of course, if you're dealing with a serious drug or alcohol addiction, the best time to address that is always now—but if you're thinking about giving up caffeine, canceling your favorite streaming platform, quitting smoking, going vegan, or otherwise upgrading your daily habits, you'll definitely want to wait on that.

While my work ethic was not on the level of my first semester, I still put in the work: I attended bar review courses, studied in the USD library, made flashcards, covered my apartment in Post-it notes, and took timed practice exams. I applied myself and put in the hours, but I definitely could have worked harder. The burnout from my 3L year followed me into the bar review.

One day, I ditched the bar review course because the surf conditions were good, and paddled out at the Ocean Beach pier. Upon exiting the water, I noticed a sign on the beach advising people to stay out of the water because the water was contaminated. (This happens all the time in San Diego.) I was then laid out for a couple of days with a super-fun bout of *E. coli* sickness.

Avoiding sewage surfing is obviously smart. But I'll also advise you to avoid any activity that might sideline you with injury or sickness. Save the bungee jumping, rock climbing, scuba diving, or roadside taco stand adventures until *after* you've taken the bar. Injury and illness can happen to anyone, but be mindful to reduce your risk where and when you can.

In the days leading up to the exam in July, I was a ball of nervous energy, and I couldn't sleep. (Periods of intense work still have that effect on me today.) The day before the bar exam, I found an acupuncturist near my home and made an appointment. I had never tried acupuncture before, but I was desperate for sleep and knew that taking sleep meds would fog up my brain and harm my test performance. I explained my situation to the practitioner, and she hit all the right pressure points. I loved the experience and fell asleep on the table. An hour later, I walked out feeling centered and calm—to the point where I felt like I could witness a car accident and my blood pressure wouldn't spike. I felt like I was walking on marshmallows. The practitioner said the calmness would last a few days—which was exactly what I needed.

I've since become a big proponent of acupuncture and recommend it to anyone, particularly law students. I haven't had another mellowing experience quite as intense as that first one, but regular treatments have been a godsend when it comes to regulating my nervous system and managing my stress.

In the days before the exam begins, I strongly advise you to treat yourself to an acupuncture session, a deep-tissue massage, or any activity that calms your nervous system and restores your equilibrium.

During the three days of the bar exam (it has since been reduced to two days in California), I felt totally calm and could not be rattled. This helped me maintain my focus, and improved both my memory and my analysis. Before the exam began, I recall sitting in a massive room at the San Diego Civic Center and watching with detached amusement as people frantically flipped through their outlines and flashcards. I chuckled at the futility of such last-minute cramming, and just stared ahead and breathed deeply. I was as prepared as I could be. Yes, I could have worked harder—but as Professor Ehrlich taught in orientation, I had been studying for the bar exam since my first semester as a scared 1L. I had been preparing for this moment for three years, not three months. Now, it was just a matter of execution.

Last year, I was setting up my workspace at the counsel table at the beginning of a trial, and found myself to be a nervous ball of energy. I was fidgety and anxious, repeatedly looking at my outlines and notes. I then recalled my experience during the bar exam, and channeled that version of myself from twenty years prior. I stopped fidgeting, stared straight ahead, breathed deeply, and told myself, "You've got this. You've been preparing for this for years." It worked.

Financing

I enrolled in a bar review course immediately upon graduating from USD in spring 2003. I won't disclose the name of the service I used because I'm not making endorsements here, but "ubiquitous" is an appropriate adjective for this company. They had promotional tables around campus near the end of every semester, and everyone on campus knew who they were. No research was needed.

Bar exam lenders also had tables around campus; this was necessary because the bar review course is not an accredited university, so student loans cannot be used to pay tuition for bar prep courses. I had to take "bar loan" from one of these private lenders. The total loan was around $7,000. It covered the $3,000 tuition and the bar exam fee itself, with a bit left over for living expenses. As of 2024, the fee to sit for the California bar exam is $850—so you may need to take a larger loan than I did if you want actual support with groceries and gas costs.

The interest rate on my bar loan was much higher than my student loans, which I consolidated immediately upon graduation. Unlike the bar loan, you can defer payments on your student loans, so repaying the bar loan took priority over other debts. I paid this note down aggressively and zeroed out the balance a few years after graduating.

Preparation Time

You treated your law school studies like a full-time job, and you should bring the same approach to bar study. Get out of the house if possible, and find a quiet, distraction-free place to study.

When I was studying for the bar in 2003, I owned a flip phone (as smartphones weren't around yet), and my phone couldn't go online. There was no such thing as social media, so I had many fewer distractions than most people face today. Even for me, silencing my phone and putting it in my bag, out of sight, was essential to my concentration. I'd say this is doubly true for any student today.

Just like in school, put in the hours every day, but also try to maintain some balance so you don't burn yourself out. I began my bar studies already burnt out, which made it hard to stay on top of my workload, but being freed from the daily grind of classes and reading assignments did feel liberating.

If you have the means to attend a bar review course, I strongly recommend that you do so. It is worth the investment. It will provide much-needed structure; as you are no longer in school and can technically do whatever you want during your bar studies, the temptation to slack off can be strong. Enrolling in a bar review course keeps you on track time-wise and materials-wise, and you'll be surrounded by peers who are going through the same thing.

The bar review course is literally the opposite of law school in that the instructors outline and review every subject that is taught on the bar exam, and they make it simple and concise. There is no Socratic method, and nobody gets called on—in part because there are simply too many students in the room. The Socratic method is designed to teach you to spot issues and think like a lawyer; bar review is a refreshing change because the instructors actually *explain* the law to you.

You're not going to take every bar review course, so focus on the ones that you missed in school. For example, I never got around to taking Wills and Trusts in school (a regret), yet the bar review course taught me just enough to fake my way through that portion of the exam, which consisted of two essay questions. If I hadn't taken that course, I would have had to muddle through the topic on my own, which would not have prepared me as thoroughly. You can also revisit topics that frustrated you in school; due to the absence of Socratic method, what was once opaque may just click for you in the review course.

Exam Time

I cannot speak to exactly what the bar exam will entail, as I sat for the bar twenty-one years ago, and not only has it changed since then but there are variances among the states. However, I can give you a general idea of what to expect.

You will likely see one full day of multiple-choice questions in what is called the Multistate Bar Exam, and another day of essay questions. My exam also had a practical component, where I had to write a memo analyzing a fact pattern.

The Multistate Bar Exam is a six-hour, 200-multiple-choice-question grind. It's generally tested in every state (hence the title). You've taken many real and practice exams that involve multiple-choice, so you should be a pro at this by now, but

I'll reiterate some key advice here. As with law school exams, the bar exam's multiple-choice questions require a process of deduction, wherein you cross out incorrect answers, narrow it down to plausibly correct answers, and hope for the best. If you are stumped by a question and have spent more than a couple of minutes on it, circle it in your exam booklet and move on to the next fact pattern. Then, go back and complete the tough questions at the end.

The essay exams involve another six-hour day, and the topics rotate. Some core topics—like Civ Pro, Real Property, Torts, Criminal Law/Procedure, Evidence, and Contracts—appear on every exam. Other topics, including Wills and Trusts, UCC Sales, Remedies, Constitutional Law, Corporations, and Community Property, are rotated in and out.

On both days, you should expect a three-hour morning session, a lunch break, and a three-hour afternoon session. During your breaks, you will almost certainly run into people you know. I want to advise you to just avoid people altogether, but hundreds of exam-takers spilling into the street during the break can make it hard to find a quiet place. Your strongest defense for your mental peace and confidence is a prior agreement (even if only with yourself) that certain topics are strictly off-limits. I went to lunch with a group of friends, but I regretted it the moment the conversation turned to, "What answer did you pick on that Civ Pro question?" If you choose to eat lunch in the company of your fellow JDs, do not partake in such conversations. Talk about *anything* besides the law or how you answered a given question. There is nothing to be gained in these conversations, so if someone goes there, say, "This topic is a bad idea," and change the subject. Even better, agree in advance with your friends that you are not going to discuss or debate the law or engage in postmortem debates.

You'll all be less stressed as a result.

Also, I've recommended in previous chapters that you use earplugs while test-taking, and the same applies here. Earplugs will drown out the noise and help you focus. The sounds of hundreds of people flipping through exam booklets, typing, and getting up for restroom breaks can be very distracting. Fortunately, you've already endured six final exam seasons, plus a few mid-terms, so you should be a seasoned test-taker by now. Whatever you did during law school exams to block out distraction and retain focus, do the same thing for the bar. This is not the time to experiment with new techniques or methods. (Except for acupuncture. You should definitely do that!)

Post-Exam

As with law school exams, do your best to put the experience and your performance out of your head the minute the exam is over. You can't do anything to change your exam, so just turn the page and get on with your life.

After my own bar exam, I took a road trip to Las Vegas with a friend and watched the sun rise after an all-nighter. Then, I continued working at the same firm where I'd been clerking during law school, and waited. And waited. And waited. Any job offers I had hinged on my bar exam results, so I could only spin my wheels in a state of limbo. It was a bit unsettling.

Finally, in November 2003, four months after I stepped into the testing room, I was finally able to check my score online. I logged into my account, waited what felt like twenty-seven minutes for the loading wheel to stop spinning, and saw my results. It's hard to describe the rush of elation that went through me when I saw the following message: *This name appears on the Pass list.* All my hard work had paid off. I could finally break out of the holding pattern I'd been in and start my career as a lawyer. A few months later I got to second-chair a bench trial on a real estate fraud case, and my entire career opened up in front of me.

You, too, will have to wait several months to get your exam results. This can be a stressful time, so don't make too many plans or think too much about the future. Give yourself time to rest. This is a great time to blow off steam and take that trip you've been putting off. You just endured the bar exam and three years of law school. You've earned a reprieve. This is also a great time to address those lifestyle changes you deferred until after the bar exam. Assuming you pass the bar and get a job, you'll be working hard and proving yourself all too soon, and you won't have much time for travel and hobbies.

When your test results become available, take some deep breaths and log into your own account. If you've passed, you'll likely get a simple notice, like I did. You'll never know if you crushed it or you barely scraped by—but that's fine, because it doesn't matter. There is no ranking or bell curve in the real world of legal practice.

If you didn't pass, you will see your score. This will tell you how close you came. Hopefully, if you didn't pass, you were only a few points under and can retake the exam with this in mind. Regardless, don't throw in the towel because of a bad exam. (Those student loans also must be repaid whether you pass the bar or not, so keep trying until you pass!)

If you do find yourself needing to retake the bar exam, be sure to apply yourself to your studies with the same (or greater) dedication you displayed in the first round. I think one reason people have a lower chance of passing the bar on their second, third, or fourth try is the passage of time since they were immersed in the material as law students. The longer you've been a graduate, and the more you must respond to life happening around you, the further removed you get from the material. So, by the time they get back into the exam room, far less of the important material is fresh in their minds. Always study like it's your first exam as a 1L. You invested three years of your life as a law student, so don't give up until that "JD" becomes an "Esq."

AFTERWORD

I HOPE YOU RECEIVED immense value from this book. I also wouldn't mind if you were occasionally entertained.

If this book was useful to you in getting admitted to law school, excelling as a student, or passing the bar exam, I would love to hear about your success. Tag me on your favorite social channel when you share your story, and use the hashtag #lawschooluncensored.

I'll leave you with a few final words of encouragement and wisdom as you begin your legal career.

Don't ever get greedy. Keep your ego in check, and never lose sight of your moral compass. The law is not a game to "win." It's the structure that holds up our society.

You're going to be working long and late hours, and will be under immense pressure to work, produce, and earn for both your family and your employer. The profession can be lucrative and exhilarating, but you need to maintain some semblance of balance in your life. Sometimes you need to unplug from your studies and your work and just live life, and you will be a more effective student and practitioner if you take time off.

Do not neglect your happiness and well-being. You have nothing without your health, and what's the point of all this if you're miserable in your career? If you can find happiness and fulfillment in your life outside the profession, then you are going to be a much more effective and successful lawyer. I believe that success follows happiness, not the other way around.

Go be your best self.

RESOURCES

To learn more about Thomas's work,
go to **www.ladegaardlaw.com**

To book Thomas to speak, contact
tel@ladegaardlaw.com

ACKNOWLEDGMENTS

I WISH TO ACKNOWLEDGE my grandfather John and my parents for always believing in me and for supporting me throughout my childhood and young adult years. This book wouldn't have been possible without you.

I also want to acknowledge everyone who proofread and commented on the many drafts and edits of this book over the years. A special thanks to my editor and publisher, Bryna Haynes, for her patience and perseverance, and for helping turn this messy manuscript into an actual book.

Lastly, I want to acknowledge anyone who doubted my ability to succeed in law school or the legal profession. Thank you for the motivational rocket fuel.

ABOUT THE AUTHOR

THOMAS E. LADEGAARD, ESQ. was born and raised in Southern California, and now lives in North County San Diego. He attended Sonoma State University and graduated with a double major in Philosophy and Communications Studies, and he graduated from the University of San Diego School of Law in 2003, becoming a member of the California bar that year.

Thomas has run a business law practice since 2017, serving the business community with entity formation, contracts, intellectual property, litigation, and general counsel legal services. He enjoys camping, hiking, guitar, cooking, and any activity in or near the water.

Learn more about Thomas at **www.LadegaardLaw.com**.

ABOUT THE PUBLISHER

FOUNDED IN 2021 by Bryna Haynes, WorldChangers Media is a boutique publishing company focused on "Ideas for Impact."

We know that great books can change lives, topple outdated paradigms, and build movements. Our commitment is to deliver superior-quality transformational nonfiction by, and for, the next generation of thought leaders, conscious entrepreneurs, creatives, healers, and industry disruptors.

Ready to write and publish your thought leadership book with us? Learn more at **www.WorldChangers.Media**.

WORLDCHANGERS
MEDIA

Made in United States
Cleveland, OH
05 November 2026

47671685R10143